Joy Fixes
for Weary Parents

Joy Fixes
for Weary Parents

101 Quick, Research-Based Ideas
for Overcoming Stress and
Building a Life You Love

Erin Leyba, PhD

New World Library
Novato, California

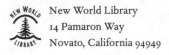

New World Library
14 Pamaron Way
Novato, California 94949

Text design by Megan Colman

Library of Congress Cataloging-in-Publication data is available.

First printing, April 2017
ISBN 978-1-60868-473-1
Ebook ISBN 978-1-60868-474-8
Printed in Canada on 100% postconsumer-waste recycled paper

New World Library is proud to be a Gold Certified Environmentally Responsible Publisher. Publisher certification awarded by Green Press Initiative. www.greenpressinitiative.org

10   9   8   7   6   5   4   3   2   1

To my kind and loving partner, Desi Leyba, who offered unwavering support for this book, and my three spirited children, who fill my life with laughter, love, and so much joy. And to my mom and dad for teaching me about warmth and kindness, and for always reminding me to find the fun.

Contents

Notice and Savor Joy, Grace, and Love

Be Wildly, Unwaveringly Good to Yourself

Follow Your Intuition, Inspiration, and Truth

Ground and Center Yourself

Embrace the Quiet, the Slow, and the Simple

Build Joyful Relationships with Children

Build a Joyful Relationship with Your Partner

Build Joyful Relationships with Grandparents

Build Joyful Relationships with Friends

Introduction
Becoming Fiercely Deliberate about Joy

You know how certain things — like snowboarding or Sudoku or knitting — seem a lot easier before you try them yourself? Well, I wasn't expecting that parenthood would be so pushy, so strong-willed in the way it insisted I grow. Even though I had wanted kids my whole life, worked as a child and family counselor for fifteen years, been a child development and social work professor, and read every parenting book I could find, the challenges of parenting still caught me off guard. The vulnerability. The intensity. Not being able to make everyone happy. Surviving on so little sleep. Having a kitchen that looked like a New Year's Eve party exploded there every single night. And the fatigue — a sneaky tiredness that crept past my muscles into my bones. The *Groundhog Day* experience of beating back gobs of erupting laundry. And the big feelings: the red-hot embarrassment when my kid was mean to my best friend's kid. The raw sadness that passed to me like a relay baton when my kid was excluded. The anxiety that squeezed me like a

boa constrictor when my four-month-old was hospitalized with a
heart problem.

I'll always love parenting books and counseling theories, but
I learned that I need more. I need perspectives and habits to keep
me focused on what's important — joy, love, and relationships. I
need tools to help me stay alert to the awesome moments of family life — the belly laughs and bear hugs and puddle stomps and
I-made-this-for-you, Moms. I appreciate any nuggets that keep
me feeling positive and well. Sometimes they're muffled by Elmo
music, crying, or a squeaky Big Wheel, but I'm always listening for
them. I need them to remind me, again and again, of the person I
want to be — and the person I want to *stay* when one of my little
people streaks naked across the yard, another plate shatters on my
crumb-covered floor, or one of those "big feelings" sweeps over
me with the velocity and force of a November stomach flu.

Through my work as a therapist, I've met some of the most
courageous people I've ever known — people who work toward
joy in the midst of immense challenge. People who unearth bits
of grace when anyone else would step right over them. People who somehow, with humility and patience, accept the tough
parts of their lives with the same kind of vibrant love they bring
to the shiny parts. I've loved witnessing the inspiring ways that
people find a way to love, a sense of hope, or a quiet thankfulness — even when things are hard. I've learned a lot this way. I've
learned the other way, too, about how tough things can get, from
people coping with trauma or loss; couples reeling from affairs or
reporting that they're living like roommates; and children recov-
ering from depression, abuse, or neglect. And, last, from working
with families dealing with serious illness or loss, I've learned about
the preciousness of life — that sometimes we don't have much

time to get things right. All these have propelled my passion for this book.

The ideas in this book are a combination of ideas I've gleaned from my work as an integrative social worker for individuals, couples, and children; ideas I've discovered (and often leaned on) while raising my three spirited children (three, five, and six years old); and ideas from the latest research related to parents' well-being. Stories make ideas come to life, so I've included many of them in this book. They are purely illustrative — the details and names are fictional. While not every chapter cites research, most do, and all are grounded in therapeutic practice (including task-centered, solution-focused, positive-psychology, family-systems, cognitive-behavioral, narrative, and Internal Family Systems approaches). Chapters align with a strengths-based approach, which is concerned not just with remediating problems or reducing bothersome symptoms, but also with building resilience, strengthening relationships, and creating more joy (Saleebey, 2006).

How do we build joy when we work two jobs and spend our weekends at doctors' appointments, when we're late for work or worried about our kid's asthma? How do we stay positive when we've had no free time and less than four hours of sleep, when there's pee on the carpet or we haven't had a real conversation with our partner in a week, when our son won't eat his vegetables or our daughter is failing math? How do we keep going when the toughest parts of our past spring to life and poke at us after lying dormant for years? I don't think there's one secret. I think there are a bunch, and we choose the one that works best for us in the moment, like picking a warming pumpkin-soup recipe for a cold fall day. When we use a strategy, a thought, or a tool to reorient us to a state of calm, humor, and peace — a second consciousness — we turn our lives (and our families) back toward joy.

Building Joy

Sometimes it's easy to forget that joy is the whole point of family life. The very moment in your entire life when it's most important to be joyful, when a cute little band of hooligans are following your every move, is the exact same moment when stress often spikes. You have little time to yourself, a slew of responsibilities, a rapidly shifting identity, and the brand-new, intense job of taking care of little people. You're not sleeping. Your hormones are going berserk. You may have lost or grown apart from friends. If you are in a relationship with a partner, it may become way more complex. Struggling with sadness, loneliness, and overwhelm during this crazy time is completely normal and human. It's because of these factors — and in spite of them — that it becomes essential to prioritize your well-being.

In one survey, a large majority of parents — 91 percent — reported that parenting is "their greatest joy," but 73 percent also say parenting is their biggest challenge (Zero to Three, 2016). Parents often report exhaustion, sleep deprivation, depression, domestic isolation, relationship breakdown, and unrelenting fatigue due to the continuous and intense nature of childrearing (Giallo et al., 2013; Margolis and Myrskyla, 2015; Newman, 2008). About 14 percent of new mothers experience postpartum depression (Wisner et al., 2013), about 17 percent experience postpartum anxiety (Fairbrother et al., 2016; Paul et al., 2013), and about 25 percent of moms feel lonely, isolated, or cut off from friends (Action for Children Media, 2015). About 67 percent of couples experience a decline in relationship satisfaction in the first three years of a baby's life (Gottman, 2015) and this deterioration often persists into subsequent years (Doss et al., 2009). It's crucial for parents to take steps to counter and overcome challenges — not just to preserve their own mental health, but also because these stressors can detract from the emotional energy that's needed to bring connection, creativity, patience, and compassion to relationships with children and other loved ones (Giallo et al., 2012).

Happiness is not the same as joy. While *happiness* refers to temporary pleasure or delight, *joy* encompasses a consistent, deep-down sense of peace, satisfaction, positivity, connection, and overall love of life. Of course we can't be happy all the time — we wouldn't even want to be. Other emotions add depth to our experience: they inspire us, spur us to make needed changes, challenge us, and make us appreciate life in ways that pure happiness cannot. "Feeling our feelings" — including sadness, anger, and fear — is one of the best ways to prevent numbness, ward off anxiety, and stay present in our lives. Trying to be happy all the time sets us up for failure and makes us feel worse. Joy is the grounded sense of peace that can always be there, through highs and lows, during a wild ride.

The number-one way to build joy is by bringing creativity and compassion to our closest relationships. The warmth of relationships has the greatest positive impact on life satisfaction (Froh et al., 2007). Joy gives us a destination and a focus for relationships. We can bring joy to a partner relationship by providing a surprise breakfast in bed, setting a date at the batting cages, or making a point of holding hands. We can be deliberate about joy with kids by listening tenderly at bedtime, pretending to scarf down the mud pies they offer us, snuggling, or having crazy hat parties together. We can feed friendships with joy by going camping together, delivering a get-well card, or joking around at the end of a hard day. Joy and love are like twins: they are so close that it's often hard to tell them apart. When you're joyful, love is easy. It flows, it's unconditional, and it's expressed in its purest form. Spreading joy to others is one of the highest forms of love.

The truest, most sustainable love stems from joy, not sacrifice. Sacrificing seems admirable. Always putting our kids first appears loving. However, when we sacrifice ourselves or don't care about our own joy, our kids are profoundly affected. When we are joyful, our kids are splashing in a pool of joy. When we're stressed, they're swimming in that stress. Multiple research studies on emotional contagion have found that it takes only milliseconds for emotions like enthusiasm and joy, as well as sadness, fear, and anger, to pass from person to person, and this transfer often occurs without either person realizing it (Hatfield cited in Colino, 2016; Goleman, 1991; Hatfield et al., 2014; Waters, West, and Mendes, 2014).

Children are more than little mirrors: they magnify what we're doing, as if what we put out there becomes ten times the size it was before. When we wake up grumpy, muddle through breakfast, and complain, "Man, it snowed again! Can't believe this. When is spring going to get here?," children respond with a grumbly "Ugh. I *hate* winter." But when we give them a hug with a bubbly "Morning! Look at that awesome snow! Do you want to put your snowsuit on?" they respond with "Yes! This is the best day ever!" We teach children how to react to a snowstorm, lost keys, or a burned pancake. If we use parenthood to consciously notice and spread joy, children will benefit from the changes we make.

When we're joyful, we build warmer, more secure relationships with kids. Early family relationships are one of the most important factors in helping children stay connected, resilient, self-regulated, and bright. Parental warmth and attachment are related to higher self-esteem in children (Child Trends Databank, 2002), fewer psychological and behavior problems (Kochanska and Kim, 2013; Child Trends Databank, 2002), protection from peer rejection (Patterson, Cohn, and Kao, 1989), and protection from health risks posed by poverty or stress (Luby et al., 2013).

Parents' emotionally close connections with kids provide a solid foundation for all their future relationships (Rees, 2005).

While joy arises from nurturing relationships, it also stems from the way we treat ourselves. The sheer intensity of parenthood allows us to appreciate strengths we didn't know we had and confront weaknesses we never before looked in the eye. We need to learn to be okay with messing up virtually all the time. We need to learn to ace those steps that come just after a screwup — repairing, forgiving, and doing better next time. We need to gain awareness of the subtle patterns that drag us down — comparing ourselves to others, feeling guilty, ignoring our intuition, or having unrealistic expectations — and release ourselves from them. The way we treat ourselves is the model for the way our children will treat themselves.

Joy is way easier to access when we're upright, centered, and balanced. We need tricks to chill us out when demands — work deadlines, a sink full of dishes, a toddler crying — pile up fast and high from all directions. We need to know how to bring in mindfulness while we're making dinner, changing a baby's outfit, stuffing Play-Doh back into its container, and singing a nursery rhyme all at the same time. We need to be ready to breathe deep when our kid floods the bathroom and to call upon humor when we unknowingly track our kid's underwear to work on the back of our shirt. The most perfect discipline system, parenting style, or potty-training regimen would fail miserably if we weren't in the right space to carry it out.

How do we become more joyful? Sometimes joy falls into our laps, like lifting the lid of a fancy dinner with an emphatic "Voilà!" It lights us up when we're tuned to the deliciousness of life, when we're aware of love, grace, or beauty. At other times, joy falls behind the couch like a lost library book, and we need to deliberately

search for it. Sometimes we need to honor powerful emotions —
sadness, anger, or fear — before we can catch a glimpse of joy.
At times, joy emerges, like a fog off the ocean, out of conscious
habits or rituals. Sometimes it sneaks over to us from the things we
surround ourselves with, like lively music, fresh air, or fun-loving
people. At other times, we build joy from scratch like architects —
dreaming it, mapping it, and reworking our plans when we need to.
We cultivate joy by doing the things we love, things that awaken
our passions. It unfolds when we're being of service or using our
gifts. It grows when we slowly get better at something, even if we
stank at it to begin with. We sense joy in moments of relationship
— a hug, a laugh, or a conversation. Joy rests in the tender compassion that follows forgiveness and can show up when we learn to
accept our imperfections and weak spots with love. It can erupt like
giggles from playfulness and abandon, from letting loose or being
silly. Sometimes all joy needs is a bit of downtime, a quiet pause, to
sit beside us or between us. Joy sticks around when we believe that
we deserve to be joyful, that it's okay to be joyful, and that everything won't fall apart if we're joyful. There's such an art to drawing our attention to the joy in our lives. Perhaps it's the greatest art.

Parents are purposeful about so much. We buy the right car for
the right price and pore over evaluations of preschools. We think
hard about nap schedules and what a week's worth of healthy dinners should look like. We need to apply the same meticulous attention to feeding our joy.

How to Use This Book

Each chapter in this book contains an assortment of ideas for building more joy, quotes to inspire you, and research that provides a
framework or evidence for the suggestions. It also includes stories

and examples for applying the ideas to real life as well as potential action steps and reflections ("Try This").

Ideas relate to both the inner work of shifting perspectives and the outer work of taking action. Whenever possible, they are stated as positive recommendations (what to do), instead of negative ones (what not to do). It's hard to feel passionate about a goal to be "less stressed" or "not too burned out." But if our goals are to harness energy and excitement, savor moments of grace, treat ourselves with exceptional compassion, feel present and peaceful, and bring joy to our loved ones in every way possible, then those are goals we can get excited about. Ideas in this book are built on the premise that if you keep habits of joy at the forefront, then many challenges that parents face, like weariness, tend to resolve themselves.

This book is not meant to give you any more "shoulds" or tout one parenting style over another. It's a resource to call on when you want inspiration or encouragement to help you be especially good to your family, your friends, or yourself. Flip to any chapter you're drawn to, and read in small doses — try some ideas, then come back to it.

The Funeral Effect

Shannon was Irish, so she grew up going to tons of wakes and funerals — many for people she'd never met. Curled up in a fuzzy pink chair in the corner of the funeral home, she heard all the stories about how the deceased person had spread goodness — teaching a son to fish, eating the crust ends of a bread loaf, covering for a sick colleague, or dancing like a fool to oldies music. She heard about how the person asked great questions, gave the best hugs, or volunteered at a soup kitchen. When Shannon left, she sometimes felt like she'd been shocked with a stun gun. She was jolted into seeing just how much relationships mattered. She vowed to bring her grandma soup, kiss her partner ten times a day, twirl her kids around, greet the mail carrier with cheer, and thank everyone who made her life better. However, after a few days of traffic jams, stopped-up toilets, and work deadlines, she drifted down from that exalted state. How could she stay motivated to take action? How could she create the "funeral effect" without the funeral?

Though not all the ideas in this book will apply to you, I hope at least one spark motivates you to connect with others more, savor your life more, or treat yourself way better. I wish you and your family the best.

Love, Erin

Design a Life
You Love

1   Grieve Your Former Life

Maybe you used to sip martinis on red velvet couches, fish in the northern lakes, or read the entire Sunday newspaper. You may have done so much yoga you could balance on one hand, or maybe you never missed a single Italian Sunday night dinner at Grandma's. Now handstands are out of the question because your arms are too tired from holding your wiggly baby while vacuuming the entire basement, and Sunday dinner is the very time of day when your toddler acts like a caffeinated chimp. It's not just the activities that are hard to let go of — it's the piece of your identity that was Velcroed to them.

If you've moved, changed jobs, lost friends, or been unable to pursue the interests you once loved, be gentle with yourself. Honor your feelings of loss, or you may notice underlying sadness down the road or subconsciously blame your partner or kids for the inevitable changes in your life.

Mountain Libraries

Josh and Teresa had always loved the mountains. They were excited about their first trip to Colorado with their twin toddlers. They had planned on strapping them into baby carriers and doing a ton of hiking, but the kids lasted about four minutes before they cried to get out and run around. When Josh and Teresa let them out, they wanted to jump off high, scary boulders, sprint down steep, scary trails, and throw big, scary rocks at each other.

When they tried biking, the kids cried about the helmets they had to wear. When they rode in the bike trailer to the playground, the kids thought hurling their snacks and shoes over the side was hilarious.

Their version of sharing the mountains with their babies never did happen. They found that they had the most fun by going to playgrounds and libraries in various mountain towns. It took a lot for them to embrace the children's library in Estes Park when they were used to using the town as a base for backcountry skiing.

Desk Job

Zoe, a marine biologist, loved her job helping fisheries engage in sustainable practices. She spoke three languages and traveled to South America, Europe, and a number of Caribbean islands. When she had a baby, she took a desk job that was a better fit for family life. A part of her ached for the smell of seawater, traveling, and being on the front lines. Zoe met with her boss and mapped out a career plan that would let her get back to traveling in a few years — a step that helped her relax about her present situation.

TRY THIS

Write a letter of gratitude for all of the experiences from your prebaby days that you had to leave behind. If something's on hold, estimate how long it will be before you can get back to it.

2 Build a Fortress around Your Passions

*When you recover or discover something that nourishes
your soul and brings joy, care enough about yourself
to make room for it in your life.* — JEAN SHINODA BOLEN

Parenthood hurls your identity into the air like a bag of confetti and forces it to settle in a new formation. As you feel that whirlwind taking hold of you, identify the things that keep you feeling vibrantly alive — your core joys — and wrap them up for safekeeping. If you swap every bike ride for a toddler birthday party and every date night for another trip to Home Depot, you will certainly lose your mojo.

Engaging in hobbies, interests, and leisure activities lowers stress, improves interest and mood, and lowers heart rates (Zawadzki, Smyth, and Costigan, 2015). The neurologist S. Ausim Azizi explains that enjoyable hobbies stimulate the brain's septal zone, which is associated with pleasure, as well as the brain's nucleus accumbens, which controls how people feel about life (cited in Zimmerman, 2007). Instead of thinking of boundaries as keeping things out, see them as circles protecting the things you hold most dear. If your core joy is tinkering with your car, block out some time to putter away at it. If it's baseball, catch some games. Although it's hard to get out of the house when a pile of laundry stares you down or a child begs you to play another round of Candy Land, feeding your inner self — even for an hour — helps you be more present, creative, and full of life when you get home.

A Thousand Hues

On Sunday afternoons, while her mother watched the kids, Ann tiptoed to her basement, set up her huge, slightly wobbly easel, and painted. The upstairs sounds were muffled — yips from her dog, off-tune nursery rhymes, her toddler's cup falling and spilling. In the quiet basement, she heard only the gentle swirl of her paintbrush as she mixed colors into a thousand different hues. When she came upstairs for dinner, she was brighter, as if the colors had soaked into her. "You painted, Mommy, didn't you?" her daughter would ask, smiling. "I like it when you paint."

TRY THIS

Identify a pastime you want to build a fortress around.

3 Create Rituals around Your Priorities

The key is not to prioritize what's on your schedule,
but to schedule your priorities. — STEPHEN COVEY

The first five years of parenting are intense. Young children siphon energy right out of you, as if their umbilical cords were still hooked up. They need so much of your time that it's hard to squeeze in even a TV show or an hour at the coffee shop. To put things in perspective, if you live to be a hundred, this consuming time of each kid's early childhood accounts for a mere 5 percent of your life. To make time to fry special letter pancakes for your toddler or play 122 rounds of hide-and-seek, you may need to work less, hire a handyman, or skip that basketball game.

Many parents' days blur together in a stream of serving snacks, going to the doctor, or struggling to pay the bills. Instead of letting these tasks consume you, create rituals around the activities that are most important to you. For example, go on family bike rides on Sunday afternoons, or have breakfast with friends every Saturday morning.

Saturday Afternoons

Ashley worked full-time, and after putting her son to bed, it was too late for her to go inline skating like she used to. She realized she missed the outdoors and felt cooped up and claustrophobic. She cut back on her four-year-old's Saturday sports classes so she and her family could spend Saturday afternoons at the lakefront. Their Saturday picnic became treasured family time for riding bikes, building sandcastles, and playing at the park.

Shabbat Dinners

Rachel treasured Shabbat dinner at her parents' house every Friday night, even when it became harder to attend with her three young children in tow. Not only did she get some time to reflect and rest at this weekly gathering, but it gave her a chance to see her sister, two brothers, parents, and grandparents on a regular basis. Upholding this tradition gave her children the time and consistency they needed to develop close relationships with all their cousins as well.

TRY THIS

Describe everything you love doing or would love doing with your children before they turn ten years old. Draw pictures, sketch phrases, or free-write.

4 Follow Your Own Enthusiasm

One dad treasures his sunrise walks with his baby daughter. He takes photos of beautiful sights he sees along the way, posts them to Facebook, and labels them "Morning Walks with Ana." Another takes his seven-year-old and a bunch of neighborhood friends on bike rides in the Blue Ridge Mountains. One mom works ten-hour days so she can take Fridays off to go on beach adventures with her four-year-old, while another takes her son fishing on Saturday afternoons. One dad, who is a chef, treasures the special time he has chopping vegetables and preparing dinners with his enthusiastic six-year-old son. When you do what you love, kids love to jump right into it, just like a pile of leaves.

Identify the ways you most love spending time with your children — like going out to breakfast, fixing things, or building snowmen — and make them happen. Children love knowing that you actually enjoy spending time with them, instead of fake-smiling through your zillionth trip to the mosh pit of a children's museum.

If your daughter likes to dress up, have a "glamour night" once a month when you do her hair up fancy, let her wear high heels, and help her try on your jewelry. If you love taking your son mini-golfing, make it a special, twice-a-summer outing with hot dogs and ice cream. If you like hiking around the arboretum with your baby, do it every Sunday morning.

Consider making a bucket list, putting your dreams on paper to increase your chances of completing them. (While there's some value in the backlash of "f$!#-it lists," which make fun of this idea and highlight the importance of living in the moment without an agenda or to-do list, bucket lists help you prioritize your passions.) The important thing about bucket-list items is not *whether* you do them, it's *how* you do them. If you took your daughter to a base-ball game but were stressed about getting there on time, frustrated because she wouldn't eat the hot dog because it was in a bun, or annoyed that she whined to go home in the third inning, it would feel like a waste. However, if you sang to favorite music on the way to that game, didn't care when you arrived, let her eat whatever she wanted, and appreciated the two innings you did get to see (before taking her to a nearby playground), then you'd remember it fondly.

Colors

It was a sunny fall day, crisp and breezy. When Kate thought about what she would be happiest doing with her children that day, it was going into the forest. So they put on their jackets and had great fun hiking, crunching and burying each other in leaves, climbing on logs, and rolling down hills. A sliver of afternoon light caught on her daughter's hair, leaves stuck to their shirts like burrs, and there was a rustling so beautiful, so powerful, but so subtle they strained to hear it even though it was all around them. Colors were everywhere, glowing in the sunlight.

Kate knew that kids love to be outside almost anytime. However, that day she realized it was her own enthusiasm that was contagious.

TRY THIS

Imagine a day with your kids when you could be aglow with enthusiasm. Where would you be? What three things would you be saying? What three perks or bonuses could make the day even more memorable?

5 Surround Yourself with the Good Stuff

I am beginning to learn that it is the sweet, simple things of life which are the real ones after all. — LAURA INGALLS WILDER

Ecological systems theory posits that you have the best chance of improving your behavior or feelings if you change your surrounding environment as well. If you don't, your old "system" will tug you right back to where you were before. Filling your space with the good stuff — whether it's hip-hop music or white lilies or bright sunlight — can ground a good mood and give it roots. Beautify your home by bringing in fresh flowers and plants. If you're susceptible to the winter blahs, use full-spectrum light bulbs or a light box, light a candle, add an extra lamp, open the shades, or spend time in the brightest room of your house.

Household clutter and unfinished business in a home can contribute to stress and depression (Kelley and Kelley, 2012), whereas a home that feels restful, restorative, and tidy is associated with lower stress (Saxbe and Repetti, 2010). One study by the researcher Jeanne Arnold and colleagues on middle-class homes in Los Angeles found that "managing the volume of possessions was such a crushing problem in many homes that it actually elevated levels of stress hormones for mothers" (Sullivan, 2012). A number of parents have reported greater happiness and a feeling of getting their lives back when they purged their possessions and provided only a few toys instead of "bins and bins" of them (e.g., Brown, 2016; Lansbury, 2014a).

Spending time outside is restorative, too. Go to the park after school or take a walk after dinner. Eat outside, grill outside, or plant a garden. Moderate exposure to sunlight helps your body produce vitamin D, maintain a healthy immune response, regulate important hormones, and produce endorphins (Mead, 2008). One study showed that walking in a natural setting for ninety minutes significantly reduced activity in the part of the brain linked to mental illness (Bratman et al., 2015). The researchers suggest that walking in nature is a vital part of preventing or treating depression. (Walking in an urban environment did not have the same effect.) Another study found that taking a walk for thirty minutes just three times per week at lunch increased inactive workers' enthusiasm and sense of relaxation and reduced nervousness (Thøgersen-Ntoumani et al., 2015).

Be careful of what you let into your life. Don't pollute your head with too much violent TV, traumatic news shows about missing persons, or internet scare stories about mosquito-borne superbugs. Exposure to negative events through media sours your mood and acts as a form of secondary trauma. For example, participants in one study who were shown fourteen-minute negative TV news bulletins showed increases in anxiety, sadness, and the tendency to catastrophize a personal worry (Johnston and Davey, 1997).

Fart Machine

Candace was tired of watching the depressing news every morning, being super professional, and always having serious conversations. She made a conscious effort to bring fun back into her life. She changed her regular music to include upbeat playlists, watched comedy shows instead of the news, opened her curtains every day, painted her bedroom orange, clipped and sent cartoons to her friends, and put comic strips and jokes in her work presentations. She told friends and family she was on a quest to be more lighthearted, which motivated them to give her a fart machine, tell her jokes, and surprise her with pranks.

TRY THIS

Identify one environmental change you could make right now in your home that would bring the biggest improvement in your mood.

6 Value Who You Are, Not What You Do

Before kids, it's easy to center your identity on the things you do, such as competing in triathlons, fixing up cars, or surfing in Australia. You may have thought about yourself as part of a championship sand-volleyball team or someone who's going to an awesome concert next week. After children, your identity begins to encompass the funny voice you use to read that pop-up book and the way you steadily rock a child with an ear infection. It takes shape from the way you cheerfully do a chore that's supposed to be your partner's or play This Little Piggy after a diaper change. While you may still have adventures, constraints on your activities force you to find subtler, deeper layers to your identity. For overachievers and classic doers, this is a real challenge.

Mismatched Mittens

If you saw Lauren on the street sprinting after her little kids in the Minnesota snow with her mismatched mittens, you wouldn't guess that she once spent two years in the Peace Corps in Ethiopia. If you saw her cruising in her blah-gray, crunchy, Cheerio-lined tank (I mean minivan), cranking the Grateful Dead as she drove her kids to swimming lessons, you wouldn't guess that she used to be her garage's top mechanic, once scaled Mount Rainier, or learned to drive a stick shift in the Icelandic countryside. In fact, with all the gray minivans out there and all the women in black swimsuits at Aquacise class, Lauren wouldn't even recognize herself. Her identity is no longer hanging on her sleeve. It's all bundled inside, like a sleeping bag stuffed in its sack. It's in the here and now — in the patient way she sits with her son who is crying, in the thoughtful meal she brings to a friend confined to bed rest, and in the playful tone she uses to get her daughter to load the car.

TRY THIS

Think of a single moment — maybe passionately singing "Take Me Out to the Ball Game" to lull your toddler to sleep — that shows how your interactions with your family reflect a deeper layer of your identity: being, not doing.

7 Set Specific, Strong Intentions

Identifying exactly what you want your life to look like helps you get there faster. You can do this through reflecting, setting goals, daydreaming, talking, writing, drawing, or reading. There is power in both the ebb — dreaming, meditating, and envisioning — and the flow — taking concrete steps toward your goals. Intentions are more effective when they are specific ("I want to throw out all the expired food") and strong ("I strongly intend to clean the closet!"). "Implementation intentions," which spell out "When X happens, I will do Y!" are especially effective because they help you anticipate situational cues that can alert you to respond in the way you desire. They help you identify where, when, and how you will work to implement goals, making it more likely that you'll attain them (Gollwitzer, 1999).

The following are examples of implementation intentions:

When my toddler skips his nap, I will take him for a walk
outside and refuse to let it ruin our day.

When I feel anxious about my baby's health, I will write in
a journal and call my sister.

When my partner walks in the door, I will give her a huge
kiss on the lips.

Would You Like Another?

*Amber noticed that when she met her friends for drinks, she drank more
cocktails than she meant to, which made it tough to get up with her kids
the next day. She set the intention that when she heard the cue, "Would
you like another?," she would answer, "No, thank you." It became
easier to say no when she had planned to do it ahead of time.*

The simplest way to use intention is to choose single words to alert
your mind to a daily priority and help you organically, spontaneously strengthen your commitment to it. Sample intention words
include *friendly, gratitude, greetings, playful, quiet, smile, optimism,
kind, present, music,* and *listen.* In their book *Words Can Change
Your Brain,* Andrew Newberg and Mark Robert Waldman assert
that a single *positive* word can also strengthen areas of the brain
related to cognitive functioning, motivation, and action, while a
single *negative* word can increase activity in the brain's fear center,
partially shut down the brain's logic and reasoning centers, and
disrupt genes that protect from stress (Borchard, n.d.).

Conversation

For one day, Ingrid focused on the word conversation. *While getting
ready for work, she noticed her internal conversation — thoughts like
"I need to get my oil changed," and "I'm worried about Mom." At
work, she made an extra effort to talk to coworkers and saw how they
brightened when she asked, "How's your garden going? What's coming*

up right now?" or "Have you made it to any basketball games lately?"
During lunch, Ingrid called her partner for a five-minute conversation
and noticed how it gave her a boost, as if she'd gulped a mug of coffee.
At dinner, she made a point of asking her kids about their day and
adored the sharing and teasing that bubbled up from the simple con-
versation. At night she spent forty-five minutes catching up with an old
friend on the phone instead of watching TV. She appreciated anew the
easy back-and-forth exchange of feelings and ideas.

TRY THIS

Think of one way you could use an implementation intention ("When X happens, I will do Y!") in your busy
week.

8 Use Visualization to Set You Up for Positive Interactions

Thoughts have a profound effect on reality. When you imagine just how you want things to go, they are more likely to happen that way. If you close your eyes, you can see yourself having fun and responding to ridiculously difficult parenting challenges with positive, warmhearted reactions.

The following are some ways to use visualization:

Before going to the park: Imagine being fully present with kids at the park — watching, smiling, boosting, or giving kids fun pushes on the swings — and feeling the bond between you growing stronger.

Before bedtime: Imagine playing creative games while helping kids put pajamas on, take their vitamins, and brush their teeth. Imagine responding to resistance with firmness and kindness. Visualize quiet conversations and big hugs.

Before date night: If you have a partner, picture you and your partner enjoying each other's company, laughing, and connecting. Imagine listening and giving support. Visualize the romantic spark and flirtation between you. Imagine the playful side of yourself coming out to meet the playful side of your partner.

Before your child's birthday party: Picture yourself having engaging conversations with guests, enjoying yourself, and solving problems with a sense of humor. See yourself feeling lighthearted about all the little details. Imagine cleaning easily and quickly.

Before vacation: See yourself splashing in the water with your child or fishing at the beach. Visualize talking to your child at the end of a vacation day about its wondrous parts, like going for a boat ride or finding a smooth and sparkly rock.

TRY THIS

Think about one challenging part of family life. Picture exactly how you would like this time to look.

9 Cut Out Things That Are Not Working or That Are Just Blah

The energy of clearing is fierce and decisive. *Clearing* includes throwing out expired food from cabinets, purging closets, giving away tired toys or clothes, going through old mail, and working through a to-do list. It can also mean strategically removing something that isn't working or flowing, whether it's a bad habit, a stressful activity, or something that puts you in a sour mood every day. The power of clearing comes from the invigorating space that's created in its wake.

Think about clearing:

- a babysitter who is okay but doesn't have a great relationship with your kids
- Tupperware without matching lids
- a mediocre TV show that keeps you up past your bedtime
- a bad-for-you snack that you just keep buying
- a gym membership you don't use

- something you do or say regularly that upsets your partner
- clutter from birthdays, goody bags, or kiddie parties
- shoes, toys, books, or other household items that nobody uses
- a meal you consistently make that nobody eats
- old voicemail messages
- a phrase you use that makes you cringe when you say it

As you clear things that create stress or no longer add value, thank them for the role they played in your life or the lesson they helped you learn. Identify their ideal replacement. If you quit a basketball league, send a thank-you note to the coach and use the time for long bike rides instead. If you quit a volunteer position you never liked, look for a way to give service in a way that does animate you.

Push-Ups for a Screwup

It was the first day of tae kwon do, so the parents got to watch. One five-year-old kid was not listening, jumping around, interrupting, and having trouble waiting his turn. The instructor warned that kid that if he interrupted again, he would make the whole class do push-ups. His dad felt that to punish and embarrass a kid that young for a lack of impulse control was harsh, so he pulled him from the class immediately.

When You Start to Get Negative, It's Time to Move On

Kaley was an architect at a Boston firm with a tense, high-pressure environment when she had her children. Kaley worked long hours training the newer architects, making plans, and solving problems. One day, she came home, exhausted as usual, and said, "I'm quitting my job. It's too much time to be gone, and I don't enjoy it the way I used to."

"Why now?" her husband asked, knowing how hard she had worked to get to the top. *"When you start to get negative, it's time to move on,"* she answered. One month later she started a lower-paying job at a more reasonable firm, and her family moved to a smaller place.

TRY THIS

Identify one physical aspect of your life that could use some serious clearing. Imagine how the space would look if you got rid of every superfluous thing.

Identify an emotion that you need to clear (such as guilt, fear, or anger). Picture yourself releasing it into fire, air, water, or earth.

10 Rebel against Shoulds

Remember that you have a choice not to do many things that seem mandatory.

Summer Turnaround

Even though Cara, a teacher, got the summers off work, for a while she dreaded them. She felt chained to carting her kids to baseball camps, swimming lessons, and summer math programs. One summer, she rebelled. She and her husband built a chicken coop, planted a huge veggie garden, and invested in a very large inflatable pool and sprinkler for their four children. She refused to sign the kids up for classes, barely touched her minivan, and spent the summer taking bike trips, harvesting eggs and veggies, and relaxing. She finally enjoyed her summer.

Push back against experiences that are supposed to be fun and memorable but actually stink. You take your kid to the library for pajama story time, but he thrives on an early bedtime, and he hollers like mad when someone takes his beanbag chair. You have a kid who doesn't like loud noises, but you take him to a rambunctious children's theater, and he wants to wait in the lobby.

Supposed-to-Be-Fun Polar Express Ride

Becca will never forget the Polar Express, a holiday event featuring a train ride with Santa Claus reading a Christmas book aloud and then greeting the children at their seats. Because of some elf shenanigans, the train showed up late, so she and her kids shivered on the platform for about thirty minutes while an overfriendly, overstuffed snowman dealt out too-hard high-fives. On the train, Mrs. Claus was quick to hand Becca's two- and three-year-olds sugar cookies the size of her head and supersized cups of chocolate milk that her two-year-old spilled all over her pants and shirt. Now, Becca wasn't one to call Santa creepy, but the one who put his hand roughly on her daughter's shoulder and half shouted, "What do you want?" gave her the chills. "What?" the girl whispered, burying her head in her mom's armpit. "He means, what do you want for Christmas?" Becca reassured her. The girl shrugged as Santa went on to the next kid in his husky voice, "What do you want, kid?" They were trapped in the steamy train car for almost two hours in the grip of a communal sugar high. The next year, Becca saved a lot of money by skipping the Polar Express and taking the kids on the regular train to the next town over for pancakes.

TRY THIS

Identify a family activity that you wouldn't miss if you didn't do it. Ask what prevents you from cutting it from your schedule.

11 Avoid Victimhood: Take Assertive Steps to Improve Your Lot

Victimhood can be both pleasant and powerful. Complaining often attracts other people's compassion and support, which becomes a very reinforcing (though maladaptive) coping mechanism. Victimhood also permits you to skip out on doing the challenging work it takes to actually improve things. If you're stuck in the seductive trap of a "poor me" mentality, you ignore the changes you need to make to get out of it. Escape victimhood by making crystal-clear requests or by taking action to improve your lot.

Here are a few examples of avoidable victimhood:

Deja constantly whined about the tedium of her commute, but refused to listen to the audiobooks her husband got her from the library.

Isaac sighed about mowing his huge lawn when he could have paid the neighbor kid to do it.

Veronica and Damien, an unhappy couple, insisted they

could not afford a babysitter for date nights, yet they continued to put all their disposable income into their retirement account.

Eve hated her long hours, but bought a house with a huge mortgage that left her no choice but to keep working overtime.

Now, the alternatives:

After a few haphazard Thanksgivings, Tyrone and Samuel made a rule to go to only one relative's home each holiday so they could actually enjoy it.

After realizing how tired he was on Friday nights, Mark always served frozen pizza for dinner.

Tanisha knew exercise helped her relieve stress, so she went for a run first thing on Sunday morning instead of letting the day get away from her.

Ezrah, who watched his baby while working from home, realized he was exhausted almost every day, so he hired a babysitter to help out ten hours per week.

Moms' Night Out

Since moving into the neighborhood six months before, Ivy had met only a few acquaintances and felt isolated in her neighborhood. Instead of complaining, she organized a night out at her local pub for moms of her child's kindergarten class. To her surprise, eighteen out of twenty moms showed up, got to know each other, and started a walking group.

Assertiveness is associated with psychological well-being and self-esteem (Sarkova et al., 2013), but it can be tough to get it right. While assertiveness can be perceived as a trait of those who are "competent" or "skillful," it also has the potential to be viewed as "unfavorable interpersonal behavior" (Delamater and Mcnamara, 1986).

There are three (hard) parts to assertiveness:

1. Figuring out exactly what you want: Don't override your own inclinations in order to accommodate everyone else's. Learn to tune in to what *you* really want.
2. Asking for what you want, or creating it: Avoid accusations like "You never hold hands with me!" or "Why do you make me do all the baths?" Instead, say, "I would love it if you held hands with me at least once a day. Is that something you'd be up for?" or "Would you be okay with giving the kids two baths a week, while I give the other two?"
3. Asking what the other person wants, too: After you make a request, ask, "Anything on *your* mind? Anything *you* wish could be better or different right now?"

TRY THIS

Imagine there is a hole in your wall that you are looking through, listening to yourself complaining. Notice if anyone nearby is giving you support in response to your complaints. If you could talk into a loudspeaker and give yourself a message in that moment, what would it be?

Notice and Savor Joy, Grace, and Love

12 Use Diverse Tools to Grow Your Gratitude

There are only two ways to live your life.
One is as though nothing is a miracle. The other is as though
everything is a miracle. — ATTRIBUTED TO ALBERT EINSTEIN

Gratitude, or an appreciation for aspects of your life, can result in positive changes to your brain (Hoffman, 2015), energy level, enthusiasm (Emmons and McCullough, 2003), and mood (Lai, 2014). Gratitude is strongly and consistently associated with better sleep and exercise patterns, improved health, and greater happiness (Harvard Mental Health Letter, 2011). Gratitude is also related to improved optimism and resilience and has the strongest links to mental health and satisfaction with life of any personality trait (Emmons and Stern, 2013).

Gratitude shines a light on existing abundance like healthy kids, a loving partnership, a six-hour stretch of sleep, or a warm home. It helps you appreciate a short commute, a child's playful spirit, or a nice backyard.

Use a variety of tools to remind yourself to practice gratitude and teach your kids to do it, too.

Yes Tree

Kids thrive on ten positive statements to every correction, but it's easy to forget this when they're yanking on the blinds, overfilling and spilling glasses, or unrolling the toilet paper. A yes tree trains you to catch your kids being good and reinforces cooperative behavior. It's great to use when you are tired of correcting, yelling, scolding, or just feeling blah. The clinical psychologist and mindfulness coach Tara Brach emphasizes the importance of "mirroring goodness," or reminding others of what is lovable and trustworthy and pure about who they are (Brach, 2015), and this tool gives you a framework to do this with kids.

With any behavior tool, novelty is critical, so make some changes to the tree every two weeks or so and for special occasions (e.g., writing on candle lights for Hanukkah).

Gratitude Journal or List

Counting your blessings can reduce the negative effects of daily stress (Krejtz et al., 2016). List the things you're grateful for in a journal each night.

Positive Envelopes

Glue envelopes onto a piece of paper with your children's names on them and keep a bunch of Popsicle sticks (or other counters) in a jar. Every time you catch your children doing something good

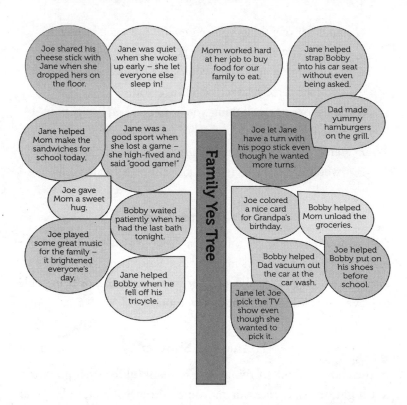

(eating politely, cleaning up their toys), ask them to move a stick from the jar to their envelope. Having children move the sticks strengthens their awareness of the times they were "caught" being good. Count up the sticks at the end of the week and decide together what you want to do at the to celebrate them.

G.L.A.D. Technique

The G.L.A.D. technique is described by Donald Altman in his book *The Mindfulness Toolbox*. It's a way of helping yourself notice good things in your life each day.

G stands for one thing you're *grateful* for, such as having food and water or having a good relationship.

L stands for one new thing you *learned* about yourself or another person, a fact, or a life lesson.

A stands for one small thing you *accomplished*, like getting enough sleep or serving meals with love.

D stands for one thing that *delighted* you, like hearing a woodpecker or having a good laugh (Altman, 2014).

What's Different Now

Call your attention to the things that have grown easier, like your baby's sleeping four hours in a row instead of two, your child's no longer screaming when she gets her immunizations, or being able to leave your child with Grandma without fuss.

Thank-You Shower

In the shower, think of things you're thankful for: that good rest last night, the bike ride this morning, a job that's close by, your friends.

"I Have" Exercise

Think about the details of who and what you have already.

"I have an ex-husband who loves spending time with our kids."

"I have a home that is close to my job."

"I have a neighbor who will babysit when I ask her."

"I have a job that gives me flexibility to be home when my kids are sick."

"I have a father who listens to me when I'm having a hard time."

Gratitude Apps and Websites

Phone apps can offer timely and convenient ways to practice gratitude. Certain apps encourage you to reflect on and record what you are grateful for each day. Others have quizzes, games, questions, or exercises designed to help you notice more positive moments. They are based on research about how positive behaviors, practices, or thoughts can change or stretch areas of the brain. Free, guided gratitude meditations are also available online.

Easter Bunny

On the day before Easter, Erik was swamped. He had to work, pay a bunch of bills, buy groceries, run errands, and find treats to fill his kids' Easter baskets. He felt the stress of the day in his clenched muscles and rapid breathing. He calmed himself by shifting his words from "I have to get stuff to fill the Easter baskets" to "I get to be the Easter Bunny! I have the children I wanted, and now I get to be their Easter Bunny."

Stare Down

One morning, Kirah rushed her almost-four-year-old child to the doctor when she stuck a googly eye in her nose while busy with a craft project. After trying a number of creative procedures, the doctor finally fished it out. As the googly eye stared at Kirah from the exam table, she tried not to focus on the stress, her messed-up day, or her guilt. Instead, she took a moment to appreciate her child's curious, adventurous spirit and the way she pounced on life. This child was the type to mix sand, mud, and snow to decorate pinecones, jump off very high forts she made herself, make up loud songs about everything — and stick a googly eye up her nose just to "see if it would fit." This child filled Kirah's life with passion and excitement, even if said passion meant occasional trips to urgent care.

TRY THIS

Put a sticky note with the word *thankful* on your fridge, car dashboard, cubicle, or pillow; set a daily phone alarm to remind you to be thankful; use a gratitude app; or frame a quote about gratitude for your desk.

13 Apply Successive Approximations When Gratitude Is Tough

Gratitude is a catch-22. It's one of the most effective means to free yourself from being stuck in an annoyed, sad, disappointed, or angry space. But when you need it the most, it's elusive and hard to access. *Shaping* is a technique in behaviorism that uses small and manageable successive approximations — incremental baby steps — to achieve a result. If you want to exercise, but your baby screams every time you push her in her stroller, you might tell yourself, "An eight-minute walk, that's better than nothing." If your child hates swimming lessons, focus on small achievements: "My child put her face in the water, I'll take it."

New Eyes

Richard hated his bosses. He found them mean and arrogant, and he felt whipped around by them. He met an old friend for lunch and started going on about all the ways his bosses had wronged him, with all the gory details. His friend interrupted. "Wait, do you like this job?" he asked.

"Yes, I love my job," Richard replied.

"Here, if you took everything that you do and you put it on this piece of paper, how much do you interact with your bosses?"

"Um, about 10 percent. Another 10 percent of the time I'm doing their ridiculous paperwork and sitting in their stupid meetings."

"You mean to tell me that you have a job that you 80 percent love? That is an amazing job compared to most people in the world. Most people think 95 percent of their job is crap, if they even have a job."

That one conversation was all it took for Richard to put the annoying 20 percent of his job into perspective. He refocused and began to appreciate the other 80 percent, where he got to make a difference and do something he believed in.

TRY THIS

Think of something you're unhappy or sour about. If you mustered a small amount of gratitude for *something* about the situation, maybe just 5 percent, what would it be?

14 Give Creative Thank-Yous

Researchers found that people who were asked to write and personally deliver a letter of gratitude to someone who had never been properly thanked for an act of kindness immediately showed a huge increase in their own happiness, which persisted for a whole month (Seligman et al., 2005)! Whether you write a long letter to a grandparent or a simple card to the crossing guard, your letter will benefit both you and the recipient. Another bonus is that expressing thanks is a dynamic form of positive reinforcement: it makes it more likely that the person will repeat or build on their original positive behavior.

In bed, whisper "Thank you" to your partner for all they've done that day. Thank the pediatrician for being a good listener, or Grandma for babysitting. Thank your child's teacher for being patient when he came down with the flu during math class or your sister for passing on hand-me-downs. Keep a stack of thank-you cards and write one at least once a week for small acts of kindness.

You can invite your kids to help you:

"Let's send a thank-you card to Leah for giving us her old
     scooter."
"Let's send a thank-you card to Grandma for bringing
     over that Kwanzaa craft project for us to do."
"Let's make Daddy a thank-you card for taking us to the
     soccer game this weekend."
"Let's thank Sarah for hosting such a fun birthday party."

Here are a few ways to make thank-yous even more meaningful:

Add details. Instead of just saying, "Thanks for babysitting," say,
"Thanks for bringing over banana bread when you babysat, reading those books in such a funny way, and playing soccer with the
kids." Instead of "Thanks for being a great teacher," say, "Thanks
for showing my son those special rhymes to learn his numbers."

Give back. To thank your partner for cleaning the gutters, pull the
weeds. To thank your favorite grocery-store clerk for being the
fastest checker-outer, write a glowing letter to his manager.

Get creative. To make thank-yous more memorable, use different
media. Write thank-you notes, texts, emails, and sticky notes. Start
a thank-you journal or write a rhyme, poem, rap, or song. Send a
thank-you photo or bake muffins. Creativity shows that you put
effort and care into the process. Here's a sample thank-you rap for
Grandma (sung in a video, like a rap):

Thank you, Grandma, for making us cookies.
They help us feel better when our noses have boogies.

You make us feel better — like a big balloon,
And we're sure hoping we can see you soon!

Umbrella Cookies

Makia had parked two blocks away, and when she was ready to leave the school office with her two toddlers, there was a sudden downpour. "I'll watch the kids while you get the car," the school secretary said. "Here, take my golf umbrella." Makia later sent the secretary a dozen umbrella-shaped frosted cookies and a thank-you card.

TRY THIS

Think about someone you'd like to thank. How could you add creativity and sparkle to that thank-you?

15 Notice, Record, and Recount Moments of Joy

Appreciate again and again, freshly and naively,
the basic goods of life, with awe, pleasure, wonder, and even ecstasy.
— ABRAHAM MASLOW

Noticing positive moments brightens your mood and magnetizes more of the same. When a good thing happens, record it: talk, write, text, laugh, make a creative project, dream, or think about it. In one study, undergraduate students who wrote about an intensely positive experience for twenty minutes a day for three consecutive days showed enhanced positive moods, and, even three months later, they had significantly fewer health-center visits for illnesses than those in the control group (Burton and King, 2004). In another study, participants who engaged in expressive and positive writing for twenty minutes a day showed significantly improved mental health outcomes, including lower stress levels, which persisted for four months after they wrote (Baikie, Geerligs, and Wilhelm, 2012).

When you focus your energy on a positive feeling, it lifts your thoughts and behaviors. The broaden-and-build theory suggests that positive emotions propel positive actions: joy sparks the urge to play more, interest sparks the urge to explore more, contentment sparks the urge to savor more, and love sparks the urge to create close relationships. These positive actions build resources that help you cope when things are tough (Fredrickson, 2004). Training yourself to pause on positive emotions helps you build long-term wellness.

The Yes Exchanges

Shantel and Jeremiah were divorced and shared custody of their two children. When they dropped the kids off at the other parent's home, instead of bad-talking or ignoring each other, they shared at least one positive comment about each kid. "Ted really played hard at soccer today. He was such a good sport, too." "You should see the picture Tanya colored. She worked so hard on it!" This commitment to infusing some positivity into each drop-off helped remind them to share the good, despite any other challenges.

Sharing Raisins

Amelia, a single mom, had two three-year-old twin boys with bright-blond, sun-kissed hair and smiles that could melt all negativity in a one-block radius. On the weekends, she took them to specialty doctor and therapy appointments for their significant developmental delays and health issues. Amelia worked long hours at a hardware store to pay the rent in a good school district and was dedicated and thorough about her sons' care. However, the hard work wasn't what she focused on. Instead she savored their little milestones — learning to high-five, hold a crayon, or share their raisins. Against all odds, her attitude was high and bright, and it was contagious.

When something great happens, send a photo of it to your partner, or text a description like "Andre went off the diving board for the first time!" or "Destini gave her treasure-box prize to her brother — wasn't that sweet?" Send Grandma or Grandpa a joyful photo or text, like "Having fun exploring the creek barefoot today," or "Sarah built this birdhouse with her own tools!" Record cool things that happen on your phone or in a joy journal at your kitchen table. Match them with pictures for a memorable scrapbook.

At night, talk about moments of joy with your child:

"I noticed how you swam across the pool kicking all by
    yourself today."
"I saw how you shared your truck with your friend today,
    even though it was your favorite one."
"Remember when you were blowing bubbles today?
    I couldn't believe that big one that popped on my
    head!"
"I liked telling jokes with you today. Let's do that again
    tomorrow!"

Mud Pies

One hot day, Miguel's children played in their kiddie pool and jumped in the sprinkler. They made mud pies and mixed them in their toy wagon, the tricycle trunk, and buckets on the grass. "Want a mud pie?" they asked. "Chocolate or vanilla?" Miguel would take a pretend bite, scream "Yuck!" and pretend to spit it out, making the kids erupt in giggling fits. They ran around, scooped the mud into cups and bowls, and smeared it on their arms like lotion. They got covered in slop, got dirt in their hair, and packed sand in their belly buttons. The yard started looking like a construction zone. Miguel hosed them off and carried them into the shower. He loved looking at his favorite photo from that day.

TRY THIS

Tomorrow, record the details of three great things that happen.

16 Pause to Focus on Grace and Goose Bumps

After a two-and-a-half-hour trip to the very pokey pediatrician, a mom may still marvel that her sick child asked to bring home a lollipop for his little brother. While frantically cleaning the house for an upcoming birthday party, a dad may appreciate that his older children colored a birthday banner for their younger sister. After taking care of her toddler son for twelve hours, a mom may get goose bumps from a sweet cuddle she got at bedtime. Let yourself be astonished by moments of grace — the stunning and magical interactions that light up an ordinary day. Despite challenges, be awed by silver linings.

Teddy Bear

In the middle of the night, all four of Gina's kids were sick with the flu. Her feverish one- and three-year-olds were up coughing, whining, and crying at the same time. At one point, the three-year-old slid off the couch and tiptoed across the room. Just as Gina was about to say,

"It's not playtime, it's nighttime, sit back down," the girl scooped up a teddy bear and brought it to her baby brother. "It's for him to cuddle," she whispered, and he clutched it and held it against his flushed cheek, trying to sleep.

Colic

Tim and Jean's daughter had terrible colic — which led to ferocious nighttime screaming — from the time she was three weeks old until her four-month birthday. The only thing that kept her from crying was walking with her in a baby carrier. From seven to eleven each night, they took turns walking her through the streets of New York. They walked in light rain, heat waves, and crazy winds. They walked her by Central Park, past sports games, through diverse neighborhoods, and by summer street festivals. Although the colic was awful, neither one of them will forget that summer, when they spent every night walking the vibrant city with their baby cuddled close.

That Spring Day

It was a perfect spring day, with a bright sun and a cool breeze. Julie and Wendy's one-year-old in the stroller was pointing and yelling "Ba!" at each bird, squirrel, dog, butterfly, and live creature he saw. Their three-year-old twins raced down the sidewalk smelling every flower they could find. "Smell this one!" their son would shout, and they'd sniff the flowers, and then race to the next ones. "I see one! Let's go!" The kids were so full of uninhibited joy that they felt more radiant than the sun that day. They wore goofy grins, and you could feel the happiness blowing off them with each gust of wind.

When they'd had enough of smelling flowers, they all hugged the trees together. They'd shout, "Tree!" and sandwich it with a double squeeze. When they went by the library, their recently potty-trained twins started shouting, *"We don't wear diapers! Not at all! We don't wear diapers! Not at all!" They punched their arms in the air for effect, marching together.*

That day, when their kids were so centered in their larger-than-life spirits, happy and hilarious, they wanted to bottle it up and remember it forever.

TRY THIS

Think about a challenging time you've had with your child. Recall one sliver of grace you noticed during that time.

17 Relish Moments of Love

Relish the moments when your preschooler brings home a card for you that says, "You're the best in the You-Ni-Verse," or your older child gives his brother a top-of-the-head kiss after not seeing him all day. Don't forget to savor a precious leg hug when you get home from work.

The Beginnings of Empathy

Callie had two dark circles under her eyes. Her coffee cup was empty, but she felt fatigued, as if she'd run a long race. She was cleaning the living room, which still reeked of a dirty diaper she'd just changed. She was putting the trucks back in their box, the books on the shelf, racing around in fast-forward, when she stubbed her toe so hard that she screamed. Sitting down, she realized she had lost a toenail. Her eighteen-month-old, who was busy playing, put down his shape sorter, came over to her with his newly mastered waddle, and gave her a big kiss. "You okay, Mommy?" he said.

Sibling Magic

Carlos first realized just how close his kids were when he took his daughter into his napping son's room and she burst into tears when she realized that they were not going to wake him up. Her brother could make her laugh like no one else could. Even if she was drifting off to sleep, if she heard his boisterous voice somewhere, she'd spring back up, deny that she was exhausted, and beg to play with him. When she had a runny nose, her brother ran to wipe it with a tissue. He helped her put on the construction outfit and filled her orange vest with tools. When they played, she was the doctor, and he was the nurse. He was the copilot, and she was the pilot. Carlos found that when he looked for sibling moments, he noticed them everywhere.

TRY THIS

Think of a glowing moment when you felt love in your family. Why does it stand out?

18 Find or Create the Sacred in the Mundane

Parenthood is wonderful, but not all the jobs that go along with it are all that compelling. Certain tasks are the definition of dull, flat terrain. These include folding ten loads of laundry, picking up five hundred Legos, vacuuming one trillion Cheerios from the floor of a car, and driving a kid to a sports game two hours away. If you focus on the boring parts, parenting can lead to numbness, the blues, and even depression. Train yourself to find or create the sacred, even when it's tough, even when you are fishing for yet another household item your spirited child hurled into the toilet.

At times, the ratio of mundane to sacred is ten to one, like panning for gold. In a single day, you might do ten mundane things (like finding space in your cabinet for the bundle pack of eight Costco-sized ketchup bottles and draining a way-too-heavy kiddie pool), but you also might catch one exquisite moment that takes your breath away, makes you chuckle out loud, or beams a smile across your face. An abundance of slog is worth even one single moment like that.

Pair sacred things with mundane things. When cleaning up a toddler dinner that turned into a tornado, turn up the music and enjoy it. When folding laundry, watch a hilarious movie. While you're loafing on a log watching yet another kids' soccer game, get to know other parents. When driving to the grocery store late at night for even more milk, breathe in the stars and the moon.

Search for tiny windows to sneak in the sacred. While waiting five minutes for an older child to come out of school, you can read a book to your toddler in the backseat, read a book on your phone, meditate, play I Spy, text a friend, leave a sweet voicemail for your partner, or make nice comments on someone's social media page. Your time will feel fundamentally different because you committed to get something out of it.

Magical and frustrating moments are often squashed together in the same experience. We get to decide where we'll focus our gaze. What we choose to zoom in on — the good or the bad — becomes the foundation for the stories we tell ourselves. It determines whether we will deem our day a disaster or a delight.

Hotel Breakfast

Amber, a single mom, was excited to take her three boys to a hotel with a swimming pool for the weekend — their vacation for the year. At the free hotel breakfast, she felt like everyone was staring at her. Her one-year-old got a hold of a syrup packet and delighted in watching the way it flowed gently out of its plastic container onto the carpet; her five-year-old made it his life's mission to use the waffle maker himself despite the fact that it was searing hot; and her three-year-old danced to his own music, twirling between the scores of patrons precariously balancing their hot coffee and rubbery eggs. However, that very same morning, her five-year-old had colored quietly while waiting for his brothers to wake up in their hotel bed; when they did, he helped them get dressed. Her three-year-old had given her a bear hug, saying "Thanks for bringing us on vacation, Mom," in his squeaky, excited voice. Her one-year-old had played peekaboo with her under the sheets. As her kids bounced on the couch in the hotel lobby while she gulped her coffee, she made a choice: she would focus on the peekaboo, not the syrup. The whole family remembered that vacation fondly — not because every moment was great, but because it was the great moments that they chose to notice and cherish.

If you can master finding the sacred in the mundane, you can teach your children how to sing their way through long bus rides or annoying waits at the hardware store. You can model how to enjoy not just Disney World or a water park, but also long car rides and cleaning out the garage. You can show them that you can find joy anywhere, not just in the places where it jumps into your lap.

TRY THIS

Think about a task you consider mind-numbing. How would you sneak in a bit of the sacred?

19 Take Mental Snapshots of Vivid Sensory Experiences

If we lose sight of pleasures and luxuries that intoxicate the senses in the most sensuous and beautiful and simplest of ways, then we've lost a lot. — SAVANNAH PAGE

The sensory experiences of raising children are things you'll remember for the rest of your life. You'll recall watching your child stick her face in a splash-park fountain, or holding your toddler's tiny, sweaty hand to skip down the street. You'll remember the aroma of the special muffins you make and the smell of freshly cut grass on the day the kids jumped through the sprinkler. You'll look back fondly at the warmth of rocking a newborn in total darkness, the stickiness of finger painting, and the smack when your child first throws a ball into your mitt with some power. Take mental snapshots of moments when your senses are on fire.

The Snuggliest Boat Ride

Gabby's favorite summer memory was of taking a long boat ride, when she got to hold her one-year-old for his entire nap while her other kids looked for ducks and took turns driving their grandpa's boat. The sensory details — her son's warmth, the whirring boat motor, the bobbing buoys, and the smell of pine trees — stuck with her for months.

More! More!

One summer afternoon at the pool, Steven whirled his two-year-old around and around in the water, playing "motorboat" with him as the baby shouted, "More! More!" He jumped into his dad's arms from the side of the pool and floated on his back, staring at the clouds with a huge, peaceful smile. Steven remembered the hot sun, the cool water, and all those goofy grins.

TRY THIS

Think of your favorite sensory memories of time spent with your kids.

20 Appreciate the Synchronicity of Just-Right Mentors

I do believe in an everyday sort of magic —
the inexplicable connectedness we sometimes experience with places,
people, works of art and the like; the eerie appropriateness of
moments of synchronicity. — CHARLES DE LINT

Have you ever noticed how particular mentors, friends, or even kind strangers seem to show up just when you need them? If you don't believe in angels, you can see it as synchronicity or a happy coincidence that mysterious people often emerge to help when you're having a tough time. In the middle of a crisis, we're often too stressed or too busy to notice the magic of individuals who step in. But looking back, we can see how they helped or even saved us.

Hard News

Jillian had an everyday angel at her obstetrician's office. The nurse had an incredibly compassionate way of telling her the very hard news that she had had a miscarriage. The nurse explained things with such care and such a loving presence that Jillian felt cared for even when she was completely devastated. For years, she remembered that nurse's gentleness as she explained what had happened and held kind space for all Jillian's questions and feelings.

Perfect Babysitter

Elaine and Amy hired a babysitter who developed a strong, enduring connection with their twin daughters and played with them in fun-loving ways. She became a part of the family and was a huge help and saving grace. The girls made elaborate cards for that babysitter for a full year after she moved away.

TRY THIS

Think of someone who popped up when you really needed them.

21 Don't Just Do, Try Savoring

*I don't want to get to the end of my life
and find that I lived just the length of it. I want to have lived
the width of it as well.* — DIANE ACKERMAN

Research suggests that the effects are different when we just do something than when we *savor* that something. For example, people who took daily "savoring walks" for a week reported greater happiness than those who went for walks as usual (Bryant and Veroff, 2007). Savor and appreciate simple pleasures: experiences, people, things, classes, or places. Experiences you can savor with your kids might include Friday evening bike rides in the forest, catching fireflies, listening to Putumayo Kids albums like *Animal Crackers*, pancake mornings, dancing to internet radio set to Kidz Bop, letting kids make their own pigs in blankets, real train rides, visits to the wildlife refuge, riding carousels, and surprise trips for ice cream. Personal simple pleasures might include listening to a weekly radio show, drinking ginger tea, reading mystery novels or Uncle Scrooge comic books, canning tomatoes, grilling steaks, or rehabbing your bathroom.

Pint-Sized Ukuleles

A local folk singer played for free on Friday mornings in a barn in the city zoo. Kids brought their pint-sized ukuleles, maracas, and guitars and played along with him, and the adults who came with them lit up as they listened to the knee-slapping tunes. Even the fussiest babies were smiling. Don savored his Friday mornings with his son — first the great music, then a walk through the petting zoo.

TRY THIS

Reflect on your favorite simple pleasures. Don't let a day go past without sneaking in a few things you appreciate.

Be Wildly, Unwaveringly Good to Yourself

22 Stop Kicking Your Own Ass

There are so many ways parents kick their own asses that they won't all fit into one short chapter.

Ten Easy Ways to Kick Your Own Ass

1. Don't rest. Especially, don't sleep enough: stay up binge-watching shows about murder or meth until you can't keep your eyes open any longer. Exchange much-needed REM sleep to examine fantasy football stats or make cutesy cupcakes.

2. If you have a hard kid, blame yourself. And smack yourself around every time you act like anything but a cheerleader of a special-needs teacher.

3. Second-guess your decisions (including those about work and childcare) over and over; burn up all your energy with excessive rumination.

4. Feel 100 percent responsible for making everyone happy all the time. Prevent others from experiencing normal human feelings of disappointment, sadness, or frustration at all costs.

5. Refuse to take care of yourself. Sacrifice everything to be a pristine yet overburdened martyr.

6. Compare yourself to everyone who steps into your line of sight or wanders across your Facebook screen.

7. Put savage pressure on yourself to be perfect and never screw up.

8. Take everything too seriously. Pay obsessively close attention to your child's achievements, like learning to drink from a cup, sleeping through the night, learning her numbers, or not striking out in baseball.

9. Pick on your body. Scrutinize, glare, frown, and channel the neighborhood bully every time you glimpse yourself in the mirror.

10. Believe it's supposed to be easy — that you should be superb at this parenting thing from the get-go, and that everyone else has it under control.

11. Feel bad about absolutely everything — how you missed your child's choral concert, how you stink at keeping the house clean, how you don't read your child enough books, how you serve hot dogs for dinner way too often.

Oops, that was eleven. I had to stop there, or we might have found you lying in an alley somewhere.

One of the best ways to stop kicking your own ass is by

taking active steps to cope with guilt or shame. Research by Brené Brown suggests that there is a profound difference between guilt and shame. Guilt can be adaptive and helpful because it holds up something we've done or failed to do against our values, whereas shame is the "intensely painful feeling" that something we've experienced, done, or failed to do makes us "unworthy of love and belonging." While guilt can motivate us to take positive action, shame just acts as a huge drag on our self-esteem (Brown, 2013). Ask yourself if feeling bad about something is spurring you to do better, or if it's just making you feel awful about yourself.

One study identified five main sources of maternal guilt, including:

- acting too aggressively toward children (e.g., yelling or criticizing)
- wanting a break from or an end to parenting
- being away from the kids too much
- favoring one child over another
- the "motherhood myth": the feeling that you should love unconditionally, be constantly attentive, and never get angry (Rotkirch, 2009)

Though this particular study looked only at mothers' guilt, the findings may apply to all parents.

A Few Ways to Cope with Guilt or Shame

Name and follow through on your priorities. Suppose that each Sunday night you feel deep regret about not spending enough quality time with your children over the weekend. You keep meaning to take them to the library or play dolls, but your chores take too long. Identify a few things that would have to happen to help you feel good about your weekend. Tell yourself, "My priorities are to spend an hour at the park with my child, read her that stack of library books, and have fun together at the grocery store. I will make the most of the rest of the weekend, but I will feel good on Sunday night if I've done these things."

Identify triggers that activate guilt. Maybe your child makes a Valentine for her babysitter before she makes one for you, or refuses to talk to you on the phone when you're away on a business trip. Maybe he cries when you walk out the door or won't give you a hug when you come back in. Understanding the things that activate your guilt reduces their power over you.

Note positive achievements. Each day, make a note of at least one thing you did well: a way you contributed to, connected with, or supported your family.

Know that you're not alone. Despite the fact that all parents spend more time with their children than they did in 1975, 85 percent of parents still think they don't spend enough time with their children (Bianchi, Robinson, and Milkie, cited in Senior, 2010).

Talk to someone. Talking to trusted friends or a therapist about your guilt may help you do a reality check, have mini epiphanies, and identify things to do differently.

TRY THIS

Identify the number-one way you kick your own ass. Imagine that tomorrow this unhelpful behavior could be magically "cured" or "resolved." Describe not just what you wouldn't be doing anymore, but what you would be doing instead, if you were being exceptionally compassionate with yourself.

23 Give Yourself Mini Rewards

In the past, you may have searched for extrinsic rewards such as a promotion, an A in a class, or a kind word from others. Now you need to reward yourself, without expecting the approval of anyone else. Rewards call attention to the care you devote to your family, despite any challenges or regrets. They amplify what's going well and are a good way to mark endings. If you took care of a sick child in the hospital for a few weeks, celebrate the end of that difficult time with a family dinner. If your job demanded weeks of long hours, go for a long hike when the project's over. After taking care of a teething toddler all day, get out for a bike ride.

Possible rewards include spending time with your best friends, reading a magazine, going for a walk or a hike, taking a bath, getting a pedicure, going out for ice cream, and making your favorite meal. Treat yourself with an exercise class, go to bed early, have a high-quality piece of chocolate, or go shopping.

Cabin Weekend

John worked at a cement factory while his wife, Natalie, stayed home with their young kids. In the span of three years, he was laid off four times. Although he was always hired back a few months later, John and Natalie always felt sick, on guard, and worried about their income. When John's union finally stepped in to prevent senior workers from being laid off, John and Natalie rewarded themselves with a weekend at a cabin for their years of hanging in there and living frugally.

TRY THIS

Think of your favorite mini reward. Name one block or challenge that makes rewarding yourself difficult.

24 Take Small and Extended Breaks

Almost everything will work again if you unplug it
for a few minutes, including you. — ANNE LAMOTT

Breaks replenish your energy. In ten minutes or less, you can stretch on the floor, take a shower, sit outside and watch the birds, do a crossword puzzle, write in a journal, look through old photos, or call a friend. If you sneak in a nap, it can release stress and strengthen your immune system (Faraut et al., 2015).

For slightly longer breaks, make a retreat basket. Fill it with favorite DVDs, bubble bath or Epsom salts, lemon-balm tea (which is great for beating the blues) or chamomile tea (which is calming and comforting), citrus oils (which are good for boosting mood), or a favorite book or two. If you help your kids make their own retreat baskets, they will get into the spirit of resting alongside you. Research suggests that when your brain has time to rest, be idle, and daydream, you are better able to engage in "active, internally focused psychosocial mental processing," which is important for socioemotional health (Immordino-Yang, Christodoulou, and Singh, 2012).

Getting away for a whole day or overnight can also renew your passion and recharge your batteries. Stay at a bed-and-breakfast, visit a friend, go on a girls' or guys' trip, or spend some time on your own. Take it very easy: one research study found that passive vacation activities, including relaxing, savoring downtime, and sleeping, had greater and more lasting effects on health and well-being than other activities (De Bloom, Geurts, and Kompier, 2013).

Mine Cozy Spot

Leah's two-year-old daughter Chantel was in a doozy of a mood. She woke up cranky from her too-short nap and was curled in a ball under the dining-room table. It occurred to Leah that for Chantel, things felt like a bit much that day. "It looks like you want to be cozy — do you want me to make you a cozy spot?" Leah asked. "Yes," Chantel sniffled. They got a bunch of blankets, a pillow, and Chantel's two favorite baby dolls and built a fort between the changing table and the gate. "This is mine cozy spot," Chantel grinned, peeking out from under one of the hanging blankets. As she played happily in there, it occurred to Leah that she too needed a spot to regenerate, rest, and hide out sometimes.

Thirty Minutes

After two months of working the night shift as a cashier at a twenty-four-hour superstore during the holiday season, then taking care of her two daughters all day, Lynn was beyond exhausted. Every day she felt like she was pulling a rabbit out of a hat just getting everything done. She made a conscious choice that instead of being productive during her girls' afternoon nap, she would use thirty minutes to rest. She drank a cup of tea, read a magazine, watched a show, or just lay in her bed for a while. That small bit of focused rest helped her regain some energy.

TRY THIS

Think of two mini breaks (taking ten minutes or less) that you can fit into your day tomorrow. Think of one longer retreat and estimate how long it will be before you can make it happen.

25 Honor, Be With, and Express Feelings

It's hard to hang out with the truth of what we're feeling.
We may sincerely intend to pause and be mindful
whenever a crisis arises, or whenever we feel stuck and confused,
but our conditioning to react, escape, or become possessed
by emotion is very strong. — TARA BRACH

While it's understandable to want to get rid of sadness, fear, anger, or other emotions, they often bring wisdom, passion, and protection, or stir us to make needed changes. Sometimes we have to deal with the hard stuff before we can get to the good stuff. Sometimes we're in a funk so thick we just need to wait it out, putting one foot in front of the other, breathing, until the clouds part and we can see our way again.

We often put pressure on ourselves to be happy. When we get sad, scared, or mad, we distract the hell out of ourselves so we can move on. Even if we wanted to commit to listening to how we feel, there's just no time for it. We've got to zoom to work and pick up milk on the way home before squeezing in our kids' ballet recital and whipping up dinner while checking our email. But honoring feelings — making time and space for them to be heard and expressed — is the one thing that helps us release them. When you're sad, give yourself the time to grieve. When you're scared, listen to what the terrified part of yourself has to say. Feeling your feelings is also one of the best ways to stay present, prevent anxiety, and cope without needing excessive distractions, which often become addictions. Learning to "sit with" feelings can be a healthy process, but you may need support from a counselor if your feelings are particularly intense or if you feel overwhelmed.

Here are five ways to give time, space, and a microphone to emotions, especially the uncomfortable ones.

Notice where your feelings are located in your body. When you close your eyes and keep still, you might notice a heart that aches, a tightness in your lungs, a heaviness on your shoulders, tears just behind your eyes, nausea in your stomach, or a draining fatigue. Describe the sensation — maybe it's like a clenching, tingling, aching, or weight.

Find the roots of these feelings. When did you start feeling this way? Last Friday, when your boss made a mean comment at work? Two weeks ago, when your child was ill? Think even further back. Is there anything familiar about this feeling? Do you recall early life experiences that resulted in the same feeling? If your current feelings are a branch poking out of the water, can you discern the tree trunk under the surface?

Invite your feelings in. If you actually took a sick day when you were sick, you would nap all day, watch movies in your pajamas, and slurp chicken soup. (You wouldn't be cleaning out closets or doing your taxes.) If you let yourself be sad for a second or half an hour, what would you be doing? What would you be saying? If you let yourself feel scared, what are the thoughts that would go through your head?

Be artistic about your feelings. Art unlocks the half of our brain that intellect tries to keep muffled. It's a great tool for exploring hidden emotions. Whether you draw, sculpt, write, or make other forms of art, feelings flow into what you're making, without being filtered by "shoulds."

Bring compassion to your feelings. It's often not the negative feelings that are the issue as much as our reaction to them. "I shouldn't be so anxious. There's nothing to worry about." "I should snap out of this." Instead of scolding or talking yourself out of feelings, summon kindness.

TRY THIS

Journal for exactly five minutes — set a timer and write about absolutely any thoughts and feelings for the entire time. Surrender to the page — let words flow without any filters. When the timer stops, read through what you wrote, and ask yourself if you need another five minutes to express anything else. When you're done, read through what you wrote to see which feelings need your attention.

26 Find the Root Cause of Your Feelings

One core role of parenting is to help kids identify, express, and solve problems through their emotions. This is the foundation of emotional intelligence (EI). Recognizing your own emotions is an important first step toward helping children understand theirs.

Be aware of the roots of difficult feelings, like the following common challenges:

Osmosis: Remember that TV segment where a woman burned her hand on a pot, and her sister living two thousand miles away felt a burn on her own hand because of their strong connection? Parents often feel what their kids feel, sometimes even more intensely than the kids. They feel it when their child doesn't get invited to a friend's birthday party, fails at riding a bike, or has the new-school jitters. Being tuned in to your kids' feelings can wear on you. One study showed that empathic parents who helped their children regulate emotions showed higher degrees of physical inflammation than nonempathic parents, likely because of a buildup of stress (Manczak, DeLongis, and Chen, 2016). Notice when you take on your kids' feelings, as if you're carrying them around in a backpack. Instead, try holding space for them, as if you're letting them rest in a wheelbarrow at your feet.

The feeling of disappointing others: It's often easier to give in than to hold a boundary with all your might. Notice what happens to *you* when you say, "No, you can't have a cookie," or "You can't go to your friend's house." When kids cry, scowl, yell, or have "sad eyes," what feeling comes up in you? We know we would fail to prepare kids for real life if we never said no and that it's more important to help them manage their reactions than to make them happy all the time. But sometimes kids' in-the-moment outbursts make us feel awful and angry, too.

The fear of being judged: Research suggests that 90 percent of moms and 85 percent of dads feel judged (Zero to Three, 2016). Parenting is a public job. At times there are so many voyeurs that you feel like you're on a reality TV show. Being out and about with kids means people observe, comment, and judge the way you do everything. Notice what feelings come up for you when you feel you're being judged.

Feeling torn: Notice the tension that arises in you from being conflicted about decisions such as how to spend your time (like choosing between meeting a friend for dinner or being present for your child's bedtime routine) or how you parent (like choosing between two very different responses when a child refuses to eat his or her vegetables). These inner conflicts may generate frustration, anger, or sadness.

Exhaustion: When you're frazzled by your kids' behavior, ask, "What percentage of my mood is due to exhaustion, sleep deprivation, or having little time for myself?"

TRY THIS

Ask yourself what comes up for you — thoughts and feelings — when you say no to something your child really wants and he or she cries loudly about it.

27 Dissipate Negative Energy

Negative energy can affect you when you spend time with people who are condescending, snappy, or apathetic; when your feelings are hurt; or when you're overwhelmed by impossible circumstances, like a boss expecting you to work fourteen-hour days or having to get dinner on the table in four minutes flat. You might feel negative energy when strangers are rude for no reason, like letting the door slam in your face at the library or cutting you off on the highway.

Notice that you are angry and tune in to where you feel that anger in your body. Take steps to help you shift from an adrenaline-induced, primitive "fight or flight" mode to a calmer state. Write your feelings down on paper. Go for a walk, and visualize the anger flooding down your legs and out of your toes. Picture it dripping off your fingertips as you swing your arms back and forth. If you've been stressed out by a bad day at work or a rough commute, play your favorite music on the radio. Sit in your car or on your front stoop to let the negative energy drain for a few moments before going inside. Young children sense when you are in a negative space and often absorb or mimic your energy.

Doesn't Look Dented

A taxi slammed into the back of Mae's car when she was stopped at a red light. Her baby in the backseat was okay because he was facing backward, but her own head had slammed forward from the impact. The taxi driver patted her bumper and muttered, "Doesn't look dented." The police officer mumbled to the cabbie, "I'm not going to give you a ticket, but next time, try to leave a little following distance, okay, buddy?" The taxi driver nodded and smirked.

When Mae got home, she told her husband the story. She stirred the dinner with an added vigor and could practically feel cartoon smoke shooting out of her ears. Her insurance rates would go up, even though it was not her fault. She noticed that the compassionate way her husband listened helped her put the incident in perspective. Though she was still upset, talking things out and making fun of the maddening aspects of the situation helped her finish her night without being consumed by such an awful mood.

TRY THIS

Think of one thing that works well to lift you out of a bad mood.

28 Ask for and Accept Support from Professionals and Loved Ones

It is common for parents to feel numb, sad, blah, bored, or weepy after having a child. Mothers, especially, are at severe risk of depression, anxiety, and sometimes psychosis after the birth of a baby, as fluctuating hormones, changing fluid levels, vitamin or mineral deficiencies, and lack of sleep can all influence moods. It can be tough if your baby has trouble eating, gastrointestinal issues, or colic. You may need to grieve if your children have special needs, health scares, or delays in their development. An unresolved issue from your past, such as low self-esteem, trauma, grief, or symptoms of depression, can also resurface or intensify when you become a parent. Unfortunately, 48 percent of all parents don't feel they are getting the support they need when they are stressed (Zero to Three, 2016).

If you are having a hard time, see your doctor or mental health provider immediately. Individual or couples counseling can be invaluable. Help from a professional, such as a postpartum doula, a lactation consultant, a night nurse, a chiropractor, or an acupuncturist, can also be beneficial. New-parent support groups provide community and help normalize feelings. When people ask, "Do you need anything?" or "Let me know if I can help," take them up on it. Reply, "Sure, could you pick up some formula?" or call a friend and say, "I'm having a hard day. Would you mind if I talked things out for a minute?"

TRY THIS

Ask yourself when you last sought help or support. Do you have any blocks that prevent you from asking for help from a professional or a loved one? What's hard about it?

29 Activate Self-Compassion

*Your problem is how you are going to spend this one
and precious life you have been issued. Whether you're going
to spend it trying to look good and creating the illusion
that you have power over circumstances, or whether you are
going to taste it, enjoy it and find out the truth about
who you are.* — ANNE LAMOTT

Learning to handle our shame, embarrassments, and shortcomings with compassion is critical to our mental health. We may lose our cool, be late to pick up our son from school because we forgot about early dismissal, or let our daughter climb too high in a tree that she ends up falling from. After we screw up, we get a split second to choose between humility and humiliation. We pick which internal army to mobilize — the one that gently forgives or the one that pummels with baseball bats. Humility can bring laughter, compassion, learning, and a calm deflation of ego. It can help us accept the darker, uncomfortable, messed-up, unfinished, or imperfect parts of ourselves just as we embrace our good qualities. Humble people may wear their mess on their sleeves, but they are the nice ones (Exline and Hill, 2012), and they are often surrounded by giggles. Humiliation, on the other hand, brings feelings of shame. Give yourself the unconditional acceptance and forgiveness that you would — in a heartbeat — extend to others.

We may never be able to change the intense embarrassment we sometimes feel as parents. We are used to controlling our own behavior, and now we are closely tied to someone whose behavior we cannot control, but for which we share responsibility. Our child may leave another kid out of a game, poop in the public pool on the Fourth of July, swear at Grandpa, bite another kid at day care, or yell in the grocery store. The only thing we can change is how we treat ourselves in the moments when embarrassment floods in (which, as long as we're breathing, it will). When our jaw is clenched, our cheeks bright red, our voice tight, or our heart constricting, we can choose to be gentle with ourselves (and our children).

We often feel like we're the only one whose kid has ever been marched to the principal's office, peed on someone else's furniture, or insulted Grandma's famous cooking. Every other parent has similar encounters. I'm not a very good dancer, but if I ever planned a flash mob, it would be one where parents told their most embarrassing stories — the real ones, not just the canned "my son forgot his science project" ones. I believe it would be tremendously healing, that revealing the collective nature of parental mortification would transform it into music, and that afterward everyone could break-dance, feistily and to their very own rhythm.

From Rumination to Letting Go

Cara's eighteen-month-old bit another kid at day care. She apologized to the child's mom, urged her own child to be gentle and not to bite, and invited him to apologize. Cara beat herself up over the episode and felt like a bad parent. Her friend offered solace: "Oh, my child did that too, but they're just learning. They're still little." After hearing her friend's simple comment, Cara was finally able to let it go.

TRY THIS

The next time you feel signs of embarrassment —
flushed cheeks, warmth, tight throat, clenched muscles
— about your kid's behavior or your own, bring your
hand over your heart and picture drawing compassion
toward yourself.

30 Understand and Address Your Weak Spots

Healthy self-esteem is the capacity to hold yourself in warm regard, to cherish yourself, while fully recognizing your imperfections as a flawed human being. — TERRENCE REAL

One of the hardest parenting skills is to fully accept and even cherish physical, mental, or emotional weak spots in ourselves (and our children). We might be crabby after not sleeping, highly unorganized, judgmental, or impatient. We might be ornery when on caffeine, prone to migraines, tired in the late afternoon, or infuriated by whining. We often waste energy guarding, hiding, or ignoring our weaknesses, but getting to know them provides serious direction for growth.

Your weak spots sometimes mirror your strengths.

If you are highly sensitive, you have the gift of being able
to read people, to be empathic, and to develop close

relationships, but you may also be more likely to absorb other people's anger.

If you have a strong work ethic, you may also have difficulty having fun.

If you are a great leader, you may also have difficulty taking direction.

If you are great at living in the moment, you may also be disorganized and inclined to lack planning.

Don't Cry

Kenji's weakness was reacting with anger whenever his kids cried. As a kid, he'd learned to silence his emotions and stand tall and stoic, muscling through his sad or angry moments with clenched teeth. When his own kids melted down about losing a toy, feeling left out by siblings, or not getting something they wanted, he felt his long-ripened anger rise so fast that it flushed his cheeks and made him want to scream. Because he'd never learned to express his own uncomfortable feelings, it was very hard for him to help his kids with theirs. When he tried repeating the phrases he'd grown up hearing, like "Stop crying!" and "Go to your room until you can calm down!" he intuitively knew they weren't right. To manage his reactions to his kids' emotional outbursts, he developed new favorite mantras: "Kids get to be sad," "You don't have to fix it," and "It will pass if you wait." He still didn't really know what to say to his kids when they were upset, so he hugged them, which sometimes seemed like enough.

TRY THIS

Identify one of your weak spots. How does this weak spot mirror your strengths?

31 See the Humor in Your Mistakes

Knowledge rests not upon truth alone, but upon error also.

— CARL JUNG

One especially fruitful avenue for learning is our low points and failures. They propel our growth in a way that nothing else can. As we grow, we screw up with the brilliance of a fireworks finale. These low points, however uncomfortable, can give us the momentum needed to revise age-old habits and primitive responses. Approaching our less-than-glorious moments with a sense of humor squashes our human, stubborn egos to make room for a more complete wisdom.

The Toaster

Dale and Lauren's small city condo was on the market. It was overflowing with cribs, Jumperoos, swings, bottle warmers, and other baby

paraphernalia. The realtor was appalled. "It smells like baby in here!"
she'd snap, spraying her lavender air freshener in their faces. "You've
got to get that baby smell out of here!"

Lauren had watched the TV buy-a-house shows. She knew how
important it was to stage the place. Each showing was painful. After
frantically cleaning the whole house and stashing all the family's be-
longings while carrying around a toddler and a newborn, she felt like
her arms would fall off. She and her husband had the cleanup routine
down to a science. On receiving a text from the agent about a showing,
they hauled the toys to the basement and put the cradle in the car trunk.
They put the fruit bowl in the ottoman, the coffee maker in the clothes
dryer, and the toaster oven inside the real oven. Lauren always had an
anxious feeling about putting anything other than food in the oven, but
it sure made the kitchen look stunning.

After the 120th showing, she preheated the oven for a pizza. A short
while later, the kitchen filled with the rancid smell of melting plas-
tic. She yanked open the oven door and saw their innocent toaster oven
melting. Its cord oozed around the oven floor like a gooey snake. Dale
pried it out of the oven and dropped it in the alley.

If you had asked Lauren at the time what she had learned, she
would have muttered, "Not a thing," which you might not have heard
because she'd put a towel over her face to keep from breathing the smoke.
But time heals, and, looking back, she could see that that moment forced
her to surrender and accept the fact that she couldn't control everything,
clean everything, or make everything work out. It also inspired her to
get rid of some of that "essential" baby stuff.

The Low Point Quiz

Give yourself one point for each yes answer.

1. You've forgotten a critical preschool event like teddy bears' picnic or pajama day.
2. More than two people in your family have had the stomach flu at the same time.
3. You've had to take your toddler to the dentist with you.
4. You've pumped breast milk in the bathroom at a wedding.
5. You've lost a kid for a second or a minute.
6. You've developed an eye twitch, a sty, or eye floaters from not sleeping.
7. You've knowingly worn mismatched socks to work.
8. You've missed an important work deadline or function from trying to balance it all.
9. You've tried to make some healthy version of something for your kids (like sweet-potato pancakes with flaxseeds or a low-fat, protein-packed tuna casserole) and had to eat it all yourself.
10. Your kids have destroyed a major piece of furniture, curtain rod, or other part of your house.
11. You've used 80 percent of your vacation days taking care of sick kids.
12. You've used a plastic grocery bag as a diaper bag for days at a time.

0–4 points: Are you trying to put us all to shame? Go jump in a lake.

5–8 points: On the path toward growth. Stay the course.

9–12 points: Congratulations, you're really taking your personal growth seriously.

It's awesome to capture beautiful moments, but real life is full of imperfections and curveballs, a.k.a. opportunities for advancement, and we need to honor these too.

TRY THIS

Reflect on a mistake you've made or a low point you've had. What aspect of it can you laugh about now?

32 Notice Which Part of You Is at the Forefront

There may be parts of yourself that you love, like the enthusiastic teacher, the fierce protector, the patient nurturer, or the playful goof-off. You may have a part that is bubbly, organized, craftsy, or chilled out. Other parts may make you cringe, such as parts that nag, avoid tasks, worry, or mope. Sometimes a part emerges that you haven't seen for quite a while, like an insecure or critical part. Maybe a part of you is worried about everything, jealous, or numb. You may appreciate a dreamer part, the one that can imagine getting to parties on time, scrapbooking, picture-coding toy labels, and growing your own vegetables. You may also treasure the realistic part of you that can laugh when the toys end up in a giant heap and the only things that sprout in your garden are giant, prickly weeds — the part that can pick up the pieces.

Notice which part of you is at the forefront in a given moment, and recognize that although it's normal and human for different parts to show up, they do not constitute your whole self.

The Internal Family Systems (IFS) model of therapy, developed by Richard Schwartz, describes three main parts of our selves:

- a "manager" (organized, bossy, keeping things under control)
- a "firefighter" (putting out the "flames" of difficult feelings, sometimes through avoidant or addictive behavior)
- an "exile" (sad or hurt, keeping out of sight)

We experience "self-energy" when none of these parts is dominating the others, and we are grounded in calm, curious, compassionate, or caring energy. All these parts are trying to help us (even if it doesn't seem like it) and often *do* help, but they can get too revved up, out of balance, or in conflict with each other. Pausing enough to notice which part is dominant helps you step out of a reactive space into a mindful one. For more information about this approach, read *Internal Family Systems Therapy* by Richard Schwartz (1995).

In her book *Parenting without Power Struggles* (2015), Susan Stiffelman describes a different parts framework. She believes parents tend to exhibit three main parts when kids are acting out:

- a *lawyer* part, which pushes back against the kids, with each side trying to "win"
- a *dictator* part, which relies on bribes, threats, and punishments to control children's behavior
- a *captain* of the ship, who can stay calm, loving, and confident and not take difficult behavior personally

Micromanager

During a playdate, Holly noticed herself being a micromanager. She was trying to help the kids have fun, intervening and mediating when they wanted the same toys at the same times, and trying to prevent conflicts. When she noticed that her micromanager part was at the forefront, she could acknowledge to herself the way it was trying to help and then tone down her interference and enjoy how the kids played together, arguments and all.

TRY THIS

Identify a part of yourself that is often at the forefront. Notice where you feel it in your body. Can you see how it's trying to help? How do you feel toward that part?

33 Acknowledge What You're Doing Right

If you are human, you appreciate being noticed, being special, being thanked, or standing out in any way at all. Parenting is a job that brings little recognition. There is no annual review, no merit-based raise, no one to slap you on the shoulder and mumble, "Good job, sport!" We'd like some credit for not losing our cool after our kid unrolls all the toilet paper rolls in the megapack. We wish people knew that we'd slept in a hot, steamy bathroom with a daughter who had croup, or that we packed a perfect little "busy bag" to keep our toddler happy for the three-hour wait at the pediatrician. We want points for sneaking vegetables into pancakes and ensuring that our children have never gotten even a speck of sunburn.

But people never seem to see these things. Instead they see us breaking open the cookie package while it's still in the grocery cart and drop by when we haven't showered in two days. Even though our kids played nicely all week, they act like animals at playgroup, and we sound like pit bulls snarling at them to behave. Kids will cheerfully try olives, green beans, and hummus during the week, but when a mother-in-law arrives on Saturday, they will refuse to eat anything but cheese. Many times we worry about looking to others like terrible parents. We need to believe deep down that we are good parents and to understand why and how. Research suggests that most people who learn about and focus on their strengths make better choices, are more productive, and have increased self-confidence (Hodges and Clifton, 2004).

Another Discipline Meeting

Tony adopted his son Roman from an orphanage in Eastern Europe when he was two. Roman had a learning disability and frequent behavioral outbursts at school. Tony was constantly called in to meetings about his son's disruptive behavior at recess or during class. One day, after a particularly trying meeting when Tony felt overwhelmed by taking all the blame for Roman's behavior, the social worker turned to him. "You know, you're the best dad in the world for him. He is so close to you, and you're doing a great job." These comments helped Tony see beyond that little meeting room and acknowledge that he indeed was a very loving, caring parent.

TRY THIS

List some things you do especially well as a parent. What's one area in which you consider yourself a leader or at the top of your game?

34 Confront the Belief That Everyone's Better or Better Off than You

Comparison is the thief of joy. — THEODORE ROOSEVELT

It's hardly realistic to stop comparing yourself to others, but challenge yourself to slap on a dose of reality. The things you think are true about others (she's a better parent than I am, they are happier than we are, etc.) are often illusions. In their article "Misery Has More Company than People Think," Alexander Jordan and colleagues report findings from four studies that show that people underestimate the prevalence of other people's negative emotions, in part because people hide or keep them private (Jordan et al., 2011, 120). As Anne Lamott writes: "Everyone is screwed up, broken, clingy, and scared, even the people who seem to have it more or less together. They are much more like you than you would believe. So try not to compare your insides to their outsides" (Lamott, 2015).

Petrified Peas

Before Trinity had her third baby, she posted a photo on Facebook of thirty-seven dinners she had made and frozen in preparation for their growing family. "Ha!" her friend Clare shouted when she saw the photo of perfectly matching containers of lasagna and chicken cacciatore in neat stacks. "This is insane!" Clare was so tired toward the end of her third pregnancy that she hadn't even cleaned out her freezer, which had a number of petrified peas rolling around the stack of frozen pizzas, much less filled it up with home-cooked meals.

It was some time later that Trinity opened up about how exhausted she was, and Clare understood that what you see in someone's freezer does not constitute a complete picture of their life.

When you find yourself comparing your achievements to other people's, be aware of issues you might be especially sensitive to, such as:

- *things you're not doing:* "We're teaching Crystal all her sight words before kindergarten!"
- *things you wish for:* "My in-laws are watching the kids so we can go out of town for the weekend!"
- *things that are hard for you:* "I potty-trained Timmy in four hours!" Or "I lost twenty pounds so easily with my new workout video!"
- *choices that were difficult for you to make,* such as working or staying home, or choosing between a babysitter and a day care center

TRY THIS

Think about one person to whom you sometimes compare yourself. Observe your thoughts, body language, and facial expressions as if you were five feet away. Bring in a neutral curiosity about what you believe to be at the core of the comparison.

35 Grow Rhino Skin

A truly compassionate attitude toward others does not change even if they behave negatively or hurt you. — THE DALAI LAMA

Anyone can be kind while hanging around their best friends, but it's how we act when confronted by rudeness that reflects just how sweet, tough, and Zen-like we really are: when someone honks at us while we're crossing the street with our four kids; when our child melts down over not getting something in the store, and a passerby hollers, "Just give it to him!"; when our toddler is doing the potty dance, but the store owner says, "Sorry, we don't have any *public* restrooms." Grow skin as thick as a rhino's, so that when you inevitably encounter rudeness, the jabs won't reach your tender underbelly.

Pema Chödrön says, "Be grateful to everyone, for the tough ones teach you the best." She tells the story of the Buddhist teacher

Atisha's travels to Tibet. He was told the Tibetan people were so good-natured that they wouldn't be able to help him stay truly awake and steadfastly compassionate. To help him stay strong, he brought along a tea boy who was ornery and mean (Chödrön, 1994). When bothered by another person's rude or annoying behavior, tell yourself, "Ah, that's my tea boy!"

Happy Thanksgiving

Elena was in the busiest place in the United States on the day before Thanksgiving — the grocery store. Because her babysitter had canceled, she had to bring along her four kids, all under eight years old. People jammed plump, tough bags of uncooked stuffing in hidden corners of their teeming carts. They hurled precut veggies and cheap champagne and all the other things that screamed thankfulness into grocery baskets whose cheap green plastic bulged under all that pressure. Her kids were getting jumpy, weaving their kid-size carts in and around scores of people hauling monstrous turkeys, gnawing on free samples, and obsessively checking for cracked eggs. As Elena was deciding between Yukon Gold and Idaho Russet, a woman glared at her. "You shouldn't have brought those kids to a grocery store on a day like today," she scolded. The mom smiled up at the woman. "Happy Thanksgiving," she said, kindly. "Who was that, Mama?" her two-year-old asked. "That was one of my tea boys," she replied.

I'm always amazed when people refuse to take a stranger's insensitive comments, looks, and sighs to heart. They let these comments roll off their backs like melting Jell-O. They let them pop like a bubble in the breeze. Then they toss back kindness as if they're playing a friendly game of catch in the yard. Some of them even like the challenge.

A Different Side

Denise was taking her friend Maryanne to a bar she'd been going to for five years. Denise told her, "This place is great, but the bartender, he's a piece of work. Grumpiest guy I've ever met — always in an awful mood, super slow, ornery as anything. Enjoy your drink, but don't expect the service to be any good. Just trying to prepare you."

Maryanne replied, "Just you wait, I'll show you a different side." When they arrived, Maryanne smiled at the bartender, teased him, asked him questions, and said, "Wow, you've got a tough job here, taking care of all these people, serving all these drinks, and it's just you. I don't know how you do it." She joked around with him and enjoyed his conversation, and by the time they left, he was smiling. Denise indeed saw a jovial side of the bartender that she'd never seen before.

In encounters with frustrated or angry people, we have the choice of bringing kindness and calm to others — even if they are in the wrong, even if their words are insensitive or rude or mean. It's not about being a doormat. It's making a decision to acknowledge the detrimental effect a person's behavior could have on us, but taking the higher road instead.

TRY THIS

If someone has made a rude comment to you lately, think about how you could have responded in a way that might have made you both feel better.

Follow Your Intuition, Inspiration, and Truth

36 Value the Four Types of Intuition

> *You must trust that small voice inside you which tells you exactly what to say, what to decide. Your intuition is your instrument.*
> — INGMAR BERGMAN

Listening to intuition aligns you with emotional wisdom, truth, creativity, and confidence.

The researchers Gore and Sadler-Smith (2011) outline four types of intuition:

- *problem-solving intuition,* such as making split-second decisions that draw on past expertise
- *creative intuition,* such as building toward new ideas and insights or combining knowledge in novel ways
- *social intuition,* such as deciphering other people's mental and emotional states, intentions, motives, and potential for collaboration

- *moral intuition,* such as trusting your gut feeling in a dilemma

When your great-grandmother, neighbor, child's coach, and friend tell you what they believe is the best way to sleep-train, potty-train, discipline, and feed your child, appreciate the caring input, but trust your own wise gut. Deciding on kids' activities is a big part of parenting, so it's an important place to apply your intuition. Value not just what's right, but what's right for *you* — and your family.

Speech

Yolanda's daughter had multiple special needs. Yolanda diligently took her daughter to appointments and followed through with recommendations for communication, equipment, learning tools, and play. One speech therapist recommended private therapy five times per week, though it was expensive and not covered by insurance. Yolanda felt she and her daughter could do most of the exercises at home. Trusting her intuition, she decreased her daughter's speech therapy appointments to one per week.

Here are some ways to tap in to intuition:

Go after the things that make you and your child the happiest. Let joy act as a beacon for decisions. If your child lights up and seems carefree at music class, sign up again. If your child loves swimming and seems calmed by it, take her to the beach.

Quiet your intellect so you can hear your body and emotional wisdom. You may have been brought up to value logic and sense, analysis of pros and cons, and intellect. But bodies and emotions hold great insight, too. If you close your eyes and notice how your body reacts to an idea like changing your child's babysitter or getting a new job, you might notice that your chest tightens, your muscles contract, or you wince. You may get more clarity from listening to your body than a list of pros and cons would ever reveal.

Reflect on how you feel about parts of your life. Close your eyes and think about how certain activities, such as Aquababies class or apple picking, make you feel. Your child probably feels the same way about them. If you had one word to describe an experience like playgroup or the kiddie soccer league, what would it be? If an experience like the splash park had a color, what would it be?

Pay attention to signs and your sixth sense. You can distinguish your child's hunger cries from their cries of boredom. You can sense when something is wrong, like when your three-year-old is quietly pulling every fluff of stuffing out of the couch, or when something is right, like when your child's personality clicks with that of a day care provider.

Have your scissors ready. Despite your best intentions, you will get your kids involved in some things that don't work out well. You might pick the wrong preschool or sign your kids up for an art class where the teacher screams at them for not copying her design the right way. You might initially think your pediatrician is fine, but maybe she or he isn't all that thorough. You might have a nanny who has good experience, but something feels "off" to you. You might have said it was okay for your kids to watch a TV show but then realized that it was violent and mean. Cut those things out of your family's life as soon as you realize they are less than optimal, even if you have paid very good money for them.

If you want to become more intuitive, pay closer attention to your feelings. Emotions hold wisdom and passion. A feeling of numbness or "blah" might make you realize you are stuck, that you need to make a change. Exhaustion might tell you that you are due for some time off to recharge. Dread might mean you should quit something immediately.

TRY THIS

Think about a decision you need to make for yourself or your children. Let your gut rank it on a scale of 1 to 10 (with 10 being best). For example:

Play in the summer tennis league: 6
Take that library job: 8
Take kids to the park today: 9
Go on a playdate with George: 10
Go to the museum: 4
See a counselor: 9
Change from the night shift to the morning shift: 7

Use numbers to move forward with decisions.

37 Scan for Inspiration

Part of being intuitive is staying open to being inspired by bright ideas, thoughts, words, and people that come your way, and then acting on them (Thrash and Elliot, 2004). Inspiration creates a spark to be better. It is almost synonymous with passion. When is the last time you felt inspired? What motivated or stirred you? What were you excited about? What rut did you break out of? What positive changes took hold as a result of the spark of influence?

Sometimes inspiration truly steps up and shakes us. At other times, it tiptoes in by way of something we read, music, conversation, an event, or an individual. However, it's when we're most open to it (high in receptive engagement) that we draw inspiration toward us instead of just waiting for it to arrive. Research suggests that inspiration has three characteristics: *evocation* (it shows up spontaneously); *transcendence* (it brings clarity, helping us see something we haven't seen before), and *approach motivation* (the motivation to act on a new idea or vision) (Thrash and Elliot, 2004).

Here are some sources of inspiration:

Words. Do you ever find something you need to read just at the moment you need it? Sometimes talking to a friend gives us an idea that animates us, gives us courage, or makes us see things in a new light. This also happens with song lyrics, when a phrase speaks to us so directly that it seems to sail out of the music and land deep within our ears.

Mentors. Certain individuals serve as enduring sources of inspiration. Others show up to give us the oomph we need just when we need it, then disappear.

Tribe. There are moments in life when you meet a tribe, a whole group of people who inspire you in your career, adventures, spirituality, music, intellect, humor, or friendship. You're on a similar wavelength and feel surrounded, a part of a collective force. There is a momentum, a joy, and your growth accelerates.

Time away. Ever notice that when you get away, whether it's for a walk in the woods, a trip to another city, or a boat ride, you get ideas and "aha" moments that elude you in everyday life? Changes in your environment and spending time in nature free up inspiration.

Atrocity. Sometimes the only plus side of something bad is that it stirs us to do something good. When something upsets you, ask, "What can I do about it?"

External signs. At times, boulders are removed from our path, next steps are modeled for us, or an opportunity opens up right in front of us.

Feeling. If we experience a positive feeling — such as deep calm from a yoga class, a sense of contribution from a service project, enlightenment from a book, or a rush from a morning run — we may also gain a secondary inspiration, an optimistic energy that spreads to other areas of our lives.

Career Change

Ming-Na was working as a gas station cashier when her grandmother became sick. She took care of her grandmother — changing her dressings and IV bags, and checking her blood pressure — until it became clear that her grandmother needed to go to the hospital. At the hospital, Ming-Na developed an instant connection with one of her grandmother's nursing assistants, named Kikuko. By talking with Kikuko, Ming-Na realized that she wanted to become a nursing assistant too, and Kikuko talked her through how to get certified.

TRY THIS

Name one song lyric or quotation that really speaks to you or spurs real changes in your behavior, mood, or perspective.

38 Stand Up for What You Think or Believe In — Your Truth

When you stand in truth, you don't stand by and watch unacceptable things happen and say, "That's just the way things are." You don't yell. You confidently, calmly, and courageously stand up for what you want, what you believe in, and what you know is right.

One way parents are routinely invited to stand in truth is by calmly following through on rules and routines with children. This is the essence of positive discipline. Children count on parents to stay peaceful but to be firm and not waver when rules are broken or ignored. Perhaps your child brings food into the living room even though it's the rule not to. Instead of either screaming or letting it go, you ask her to eat in the kitchen. Or maybe your child splashes water out of the bathtub. You remind him that the water needs to stay in the tub. He does it again, and you calmly take him out.

Parents are also given the opportunity to stand in truth when complex challenges arise with a day care provider, a coach, a partner, a doctor, or a stranger.

The Sixth Poke

One Sunday afternoon, Owen's one-year-old daughter had a fever of over 105 degrees, so the urgent-care doctor sent her to the emergency room. A nursing assistant tried five times to put in an IV. Owen told the assistant that he would not let him try another time and asked for the nurse with the most experience to come in and do it instead.

Underwater

Arella signed up with her one-year-old for a Mommy-and-me swimming class. In the first session, the instructor took her baby and swooshed his head underwater. She knew this learning-by-fire approach was not right for her son, even if it had worked for a jillion other kids. She got the manager's word that no one would ever try to push her child's head underwater again.

TRY THIS

Recall one situation in which you've recently been invited to stand in your truth. How did you handle it?

39 Find a Way to Be of Service

The best way to find yourself is to lose yourself in the service of others. — MOHANDAS K. GANDHI

It's astounding how even a small bit of service can pull you out of your own funk. It can help make meaning out of something senseless, or at least infuse a little grace into it. The benefits of volunteering include improved physical, mental, and emotional health; lower stress levels; a deeper connection to others and stronger sense of purpose (United Health Group, 2013); and greater happiness (Borgonovi, 2008). Visiting an elderly neighbor, shoveling snow from someone's driveway, or conducting a diaper drive for a women's and children's shelter adds meaning to your life. If you align service with your personal strengths, it can be even more beneficial for everyone.

After a miscarriage, Beverly experienced severe depression for about a year. She later volunteered to facilitate a support group for parents who had lost babies through miscarriage or stillbirth.

Liza had a son with autism spectrum disorder (ASD). She shared resources and tips with other parents of children with ASD by talking with them in the school parking lot and through an online support group.

After William had had a child in the neonatal intensive care unit (NICU), he volunteered once a quarter to make cookies for NICU parents.

Tessa had trouble finding childcare for her own prenatal appointments, so she offered to watch a friend's children while she went for hers.

Shawn made delicious pulled pork for coworkers, family friends, and neighbors whenever they were going through something tough.

Fund-Raiser

Fiona's five-year-old daughter was undergoing treatment for cancer. Her daughter endured multiple blood tests, shots, chemotherapy, hospital stays, and a host of other scary experiences. Fiona was overwhelmed and fearful. She used counseling to honor her emotions, connect and communicate with her husband and child, and care for herself. She also organized a race that raised thousands of dollars for pediatric cancer research. She attended birthday parties, wellness anniversaries, and funerals for the families in her support group. She also became an email mentor for other families who had kids with cancer, and helped them build hope.

TRY THIS

List some of your favorite ways to be of service.

Ground and
Center Yourself

40 Avoid Mood Matching

It's not easy to remain grounded in peace and positivity when other people's moods bubble up, whine, or leap off the couch behind you. It's hard to hold a good mood when a little person is in a state of refusal, upset, or downright obstinacy. When the wind picks up and swirls you toward the chaos of the day, it takes a crystal-clear intention to hold steady, to be the gentle oasis, the safe spot, the laughter, and the grace.

The Pool of Calm

Mario wakes up happy. Then his son bounds down the stairs hollering and monkeying around and wakes up his baby brother. He whines about something he can't find. He doesn't want cereal, he wants oatmeal. He won't get dressed. Instead of growling back, Mario observes his son, hugs him, and talks to him quietly. Rather than getting swept into his son's crabby mood, he continues smiling over his steaming coffee. Eventually his son joins him with, "Can I set the table for breakfast?" Then,

"Can I sit on your lap?" *The mood lifts. Mario helps his son tiptoe into the pool of calm he provides, instead of letting his son drag his own mood down.*

TRY THIS

Remember a time when you got pulled into your child's stress or upset. What would help you stay calm in that kind of moment?

41 Use Mindfulness to Stay Aware of the Present Moment

*Mindfulness is: the awareness that emerges
through paying attention, on purpose, in the present moment,
non-judgmentally, to the unfolding of experience moment by moment.*
— JON KABAT-ZINN

About 47 percent of people's waking hours are spent doing anything except being in the moment and focusing on the current activity (Killingsworth and Gilbert, 2010). Mindfulness involves paying attention to aspects of the present moment, like your breath, feelings, thoughts, and body, as if you were a nonjudgmental observer looking in on yourself. It also involves awareness of your environment and the people around you. Mindfulness has been shown to increase subjective well-being, reduce psychological symptoms and emotional reactivity, and improve behavioral regulation (Keng, Smoski, and Robins, 2011). It helps you be more present and in tune with yourself, your life, and your loved ones.

Here are some examples of awareness:

"I'm noticing I'm torn between pushing my baby on the swing or watching my daughter on the slide."

"I'm noticing I'm being mean to my partner, even though I was so excited to see her after work. I wonder what that's about."

"I'm noticing part of me wants to lose weight by continuing to run, but another part of me acknowledges my aching knee and thinks I should stop."

Stay focused on the present moment and accept what you observe — thoughts, emotions, body sensations, or mood — without judgment. If you are mindful, each day is like a lifetime. If you are present, the day's great purpose reveals itself to you.

TRY THIS

At the playground, for five minutes watch the way your children move — the way they use their bodies, climb or swing on equipment, run, or coordinate their movements to accomplish a task. During dinner, for five minutes gaze around the table, noticing the faces of your children, the way they approach their food, and the energies they hold in that moment. On a date, for five minutes become aware of what you bring to the table — your body language, the topics you bring up, your reactions to your partner, the tone of your voice, and the expression on your face. If you feel a distraction emerge, like wanting to check your phone for new texts, release the thought as if it were a helium balloon floating away.

42 Use Diaphragmatic Breathing

To experience peace does not mean that your life is
always blissful. It means that you are capable
of tapping into a blissful state of mind amidst the normal chaos
of a hectic life. — JILL BOLTE TAYLOR

Diaphragmatic breathing has been shown to decrease stress (McKay, 2012) and lower heart rate variability (Kulur et al., 2009). It involves inhaling slowly and deeply through the nose into the bottom of the lungs, drawing the air as deep into the lungs as possible. After taking a full breath, you hold it for a moment, then exhale in a slow and controlled way. Using diaphragmatic breathing along with positive imagery (thinking about a time or place where you have experienced the positive feelings of enjoyment, care, love, peace, or appreciation and focusing on it) has been shown to reduce stress more than just sitting quietly (Childre and Rozman, 2005; Tice, 2007).

Another technique is to breathe in for five seconds and out for five seconds, focusing on your breath, noticing its rhythm, and saying to yourself, "Breathing in, breathing out."

TRY THIS

When you notice yourself unconsciously holding your breath because of stress or anxiety, take at least three deep breaths. With each breath, imagine pushing out toxic stress and inhaling clear, pure air to purify your body. Also, make a list of memories or images that invoke in you feelings of happiness, love, or delight. When you notice you are stressed, focus on one of them for a minute or two.

43 Do Quick Meditations

*The miracle is not to walk on water. It is to walk on this earth
with awareness.* — THICH NHAT HANH

The benefits of meditation are surprisingly robust. Meditation has
a moderate effect on alleviating symptoms of depression, anxiety,
and pain (Goyal et al., 2014). In one study, mindfulness meditation
was found to actually change the structure of the brain, increasing
the cortical thickness in the hippocampus and areas of the brain
that help regulate emotions. It was also found to decrease brain
cell volume in the amygdala (which is responsible for fear, anxiety,
and stress). Study participants who meditated reported decreased
stress and improved psychological well-being (Holzel et al., 2011).
Research suggests that both meditation and progressive muscle relaxation (described below) are more effective at decreasing anxiety
than just trying to relax (Rausch, Gramling, and Auerbach, 2006).

Meditation's immediate physiological benefits (such as lowering heart rate) can be achieved in just a few minutes. You don't need to sit cross-legged, lie on a yoga mat, or use fancy soundtracks. You can meditate while feeding a baby or pushing a stroller. Breathe, drawing your attention to your breath. When you get distracted, remind yourself, "All sounds return to the breath. All thoughts return to the breath. All feelings return to the breath. All distractions return to the breath." Try a walking meditation, where you think, "All sounds return to the pace. All thoughts return to the pace. All feelings return to the pace. All distractions return to the pace."

Another form of meditation is a body scan, where you systematically focus attention on each area of your body. Mark Bertin suggests starting a body scan by sitting in a chair or lying down and breathing deeply for a few minutes. He writes:

> Expect your mind to wander, and when it does, return your attention... without judging yourself or giving yourself a hard time. Bring your attention to your feet, noticing any sensations in your feet; shift your attention to your lower legs, observing them, and then your upper legs, noticing any sensations. Next observe your abdomen, including your internal organs and muscles. Work your way up to observing your chest and heart, your neck, and finally your head and brain, with special attention to your eyes and mouth. (Bertin, 2015)

You can also do a shorter form of body check-in, asking, "What parts of my body feel healthy and good?" and "What parts of my body feel tight or uncomfortable?" (Findley, 2014).

Loving-kindness meditation, described by Sharon Salzberg in her book *Loving-Kindness*, can be particularly helpful for bringing forth compassion, goodwill, and warmth. You start by repeating: "May I be safe. May I be happy. May I be healthy. May I live with ease." You can then extend this meditation to a loved one, a friend, a neutral person (like a coffee-shop worker), a "troublesome adversary" (like a coworker who annoys you), a group of people elsewhere in the world (such as all children who are hungry), and "all beings everywhere." Beyond contributing to your own peace, this activity can actually make you act with greater kindness (Salzberg, 2002). Research has found this meditation to increase positive emotions; decrease migraines, chronic pain, stress, and PTSD symptoms; and activate empathy and compassion (Seppälä, 2014).

TRY THIS

Reflect on any positive or negative associations meditation has for you. If you were to successfully meditate for just five minutes a day, where would those five minutes best fit in? In the school pickup line? On a morning walk? Before you fall asleep?

44 Be Intentional about Music

Everything in the universe has a rhythm, everything dances.
— MAYA ANGELOU

Listening to music has been found to reduce stress, anxiety, pain, and depression; enhance life satisfaction, optimism, and hope; and make life seem more meaningful (Gupta and Gupta, 2016). Listening to positive music may increase happiness, especially when it is done with that intention (Ferguson, 2013). One study showed that toddlers' participation in music at home had a positive effect (even greater than the benefit of shared reading) on prosocial skills, numeracy, and attention (Williams et al., 2015). Singing to babies shows particular potential to improve babies' functioning and reduce parents' stress (Longhi, 2013). Play an eclectic mix, such as rock and roll, country, classical, and children's folk songs. Invest in an alarm clock that plays music to wake you up.

Music can:

Remind you of great memories: You may be busy searching for Mr. Potato Head's ear, but those background tunes remind you of an Alaska road trip, an African drum circle, or a memorable football game.

Recover a good mood: If you are having the kind of day where you accidentally wash your hair with shaving cream or get smacked with a parking ticket, blast songs that remind you of the human universality of messing up and moving on. Try U2's "Some Days Are Better than Others," Taylor Swift's "Shake It Off," or Poi Dog Pondering's "Complicated."

Calm things down: Choose lullabies for bedtime, gentle flute music for the predinner (un)happy hour, sounds of nature for naps, and light rock to calm your family and lower everyone's heart rate.

Rev things up: Freestyle dance parties balance out the scores of times you need to hush and rush kids from here to there. Playing happy dance music, shaking maracas and tambourines, and making up crazy moves provides space for the uninhibited self-expression of childhood. It tells kids, "You're not late, you don't have to be quiet, you don't have to stand in line and listen. You don't have to share or eat your broccoli or do your homework. Just feel the music and do your thing over there, and I'll do mine over here, and once in a while we'll twirl each other." It invites your inner child to boogie down, too.

Help you tune in to feelings: Ask, "How am I doing? What music do I need right now?"

Let kids be in charge: Give children an old CD or MP3 player and show them how to work it. Rotate the role of DJ of the day, letting kids play their favorite tunes (and learn tolerance and patience when it's not their turn).

TRY THIS

Think of one song that would be great for you to hear right now.

45 Revise Your Self-Talk and Stories

You need to learn how to select your thoughts
just the same way you select your clothes every day.
This is a power you can cultivate. If you want to control things
in your life so bad, work on the mind. That's the only thing
you should be trying to control. — ELIZABETH GILBERT

Your inner voice might have a positive tone, like a taskmaster encouraging you to get things done, take care of yourself, and do the right thing. But its messages may sometimes be critical, doubting, discouraging, or scolding. Replace "You are useless. Everyone else has this under control" with "It's normal for you to have challenges. You're making progress every day." Replace "Why is everything a struggle with my toddler?" with "It's normal for toddlers to resist things. This is part of their job." Research suggests that when people use their own name ("Ann, you've got this") or the word *you* ("You can do this"), it helps regulate their thoughts, feelings, and behaviors under stress — as if they were actually being coached through a difficult situation (Kross et al., 2014).

Here are a couple of examples of changing self-talk:

> If there's a friend who stops calling you back, replace "She must not like me" with "She might be busy right now."
>
> Replace "I have such a naughty kid — she never wants to go to bed" with "My child's having a hard time settling down at night; I wonder what might calm her."

More Milk

Each time Kelly's mom came to visit, she made comments like "You really need to give the kids more milk — they may not be getting enough calcium," "You should put them down for naps earlier," and "If you put the vegetables in a casserole, the kids would eat them." For a while, Kelly was stuck on the belief that "my parenting is never good enough for my mother." Thinking this way made her extra sensitive to these types of comments, which readied her to be angry again. Kelly changed the story to "My mother is trying to help. She wants to share her experience and wants the best for me and her grandkids." After shifting her story, Kelly stopped fuming and started appreciating the positive things her mom did do to help out.

TRY THIS

Record your self-talk in a journal to give yourself space to observe it, see patterns, and identify better messages.

46 Apply Mantras

Applying personalized mantras (slogans, sayings, or quotations that you repeat) can help you reframe challenging situations. It can also help you summon the reactions — like gentleness, patience, hope, and courage — that are most needed from you at the time. Using mantras can help you pivot from a negative space to a positive one, help you ground or center yourself, remind you of your highest priorities, and disrupt anxious or negative thought patterns. Mantras work best when you choose them yourself and they are meaningful to you.

Mantras can help you reframe tough situations so you can see them in a more positive light. For example, the early childhood educator Janet Lansbury writes that when you say "red," toddlers are almost compelled to say "blue." It's part of their shtick, their development, and their path toward becoming their own people (Lansbury, 2014b). Thinking "red and blue" (instead of "defiant/naughty") when toddlers argue or push back may help you respond to resistance with more positivity and ease. Another example is the phrase "kids are little Tarzans," which reminds you that kids are not little adults — they have a developmental need for tons of movement. When kids are jumping from couch to couch or running laps around a dining-room table, and you say "little Tarzans," it might help you react with more compassion (and maybe organize a quick trip to the playground).

While some mantras help you see situations in a new light, others remind you — like alarms going off — of the things you most want to fit in a busy day. For example, on Sunday nights, you might ask, "Did we have some *hygge* this weekend?" (*Hygge* is a Danish word for enjoying downtime and simple pleasures, spending time with family and friends, resting, and being cozy) (Lally, 2016). You might say, "Ten to one," which reminds you to aim for ten positive interactions with your child for every one negative one.

Still other mantras remind you to follow through on positive parenting practices. One example is "But you can," which reminds you to correct kids' problematic behavior by suggesting a positive alternative: "Don't throw the blocks, *but* you can throw a ball." "Don't color on the walls, *but* you can color on this paper." Another is using "When and then." "*When* you put away your clothes, *then* you can watch TV." "*When* you clean up your toys, *then* you can go outside." The phrase "relationship before request" can remind you to connect with a child before requesting them to do things. Instead of interrupting a child's play with "Put your pajamas on!" you might say, "I see you're playing with that helicopter, hooking those boxes onto the string. Let's find a special place to leave your helicopter so you can play with it in the morning, since it's time to put your pajamas on."

Some mantras prompt an action-oriented part of yourself, such as using the phrase "Do it now" to avoid procrastinating about cleaning scum from the fridge drawers or donating toys no one plays with anymore. Other mantras may help you cope with anxiety. For example, saying "Stop it" to yourself may disrupt your negative or ruminating thoughts. Saying "Will this matter ten years from now?" might help you gain perspective or calm your dramatic reactions when you are stressed.

Think and Expect

Luciana's son Elian was diagnosed with epilepsy at the age of two. As a result of numerous hospital stays and a string of medication and procedure trials, Luciana developed an intense anxiety about Elian's health. When she found herself stuck in a cycle of fear-based thoughts, she repeated, "Think and expect that good things will happen, because they usually do," to help calm herself down, remember the times when things had turned out all right (despite scares), and give herself hope.

TRY THIS

Identify one of your favorite parenting mantras or a phrase that helps you react in a more positive, hopeful, centered way.

47 Pause

Between stimulus and response there is a space.
In that space is our power to choose our response. In our response
lies our growth and our freedom. — VIKTOR E. FRANKL

There is great wisdom in the pause. Taking a step back to breathe and suspend judgment provides an opportunity for our highest wisdom to show up and take the lead.

Pause to Understand What's Really Going On

Liza's two-year-old daughter, Joniqua, started picking up the small rocks under the fence and throwing them at her baby brother. Until then, she'd been playing nicely in the sandbox and riding her scooter. Liza was about to raise her voice when she paused. She thought about why Joniqua would suddenly do something she knew she shouldn't. She remembered how she had been up twice in the night, had woken up especially early, and hadn't eaten much of her snack. Joniqua was ready for an earlier lunch and an earlier nap, and that was her way of showing it.

Pause to Access Intuition

Megan's ten-month-old, Mateo, was being especially clingy. She couldn't put him down; he felt stuck to her like a burr. He had a slight cold, hadn't eaten any breakfast, and was whining constantly. Megan was trying to make breakfast for Mateo's older siblings, but she couldn't. She paused, closed her eyes, felt him in her arms, and immediately realized why he was fussing. She made an appointment with the pediatrician for later that day, and Mateo was diagnosed with a double ear infection.

Pause to Support Kids without Taking Over for Them

Filip's one-year-old, Shariq, was sitting with his shape sorter, trying to get the square into one of the holes. Filip wanted to help, to guide it so he could push it in, but he made himself pause. Shariq didn't end up getting the shape in that day, but he learned to do it himself a little later. The pause kept Filip from stealing that achievement from him.

Pause to Calm

Ashley's two-year-old daughter, Camila, had been potty training for what felt like forever. She wanted control over the situation, and Ashley understood that, but all the little details were driving her crazy. Camila wanted to pull down her own pants one day and wanted her mom to do it the next. One day she wanted to climb onto the toilet herself, and the next day she insisted her mom lift her. Ashley stepped out of the bathroom and cleared her head. She disengaged from the power struggles and could again appreciate Camila's determination and will.

TRY THIS

The next time you experience a challenging situation, pause by doing some deep breathing, closing your eyes for a moment, opening a window, getting a drink of water, or going to the bathroom.

48 Know Your Triggers Inside and Out

Know your triggers — behaviors, situations, people, or experiences that upset you — by tapping in to your deep passions, regrets, or fears. Triggers are most often rooted in experiences from your family of origin or your childhood. If you value the relationships you have with your siblings, you might feel unsettled when your children argue or fight with each other. If you care deeply about the elderly, you might lose your cool when your kid is rude to a grandparent. If your father passed from diabetes, you might be exceptionally strict about your child's sugar intake. If you had the most hustle on your high school softball team, you might be especially frustrated when your child acts lazy at her games. If a parent often yelled at you when you were young, you might shut down immediately when your partner yells in the same way. If you regret not getting into a certain college, you may react strongly when your child refuses to do his homework.

When you have a strong emotional reaction to a situation, ask yourself what it tapped in to, such as a need, a fear, a desire to be liked, a craving for a sense of order, a reminder of a past trauma, or a difficulty from childhood. Knowing your triggers in advance helps you manage the "big feelings" that they produce.

Before Parties

Robin's parents were the ultimate party hosts, so Robin put pressure on herself to live up to their standards. One day she found herself trying to frost the cake, fill the soap dispensers, hide the laundry, change diapers, and bathe her kids while making ten gallons of coffee and baking souf-flés that must puff up. The countdown closed in on her like an eclipse. After that party, Robin realized that her friends didn't care if she show-ered. No one noticed whether she put up decorations. What did matter was that she could be as happy before the party as she was during the event itself.

Apple Look-Alikes

Holiday celebrations were a highlight of Elaine's childhood. Her pas-sion for the holidays persisted into her adulthood, where she loved talking to everyone, preparing and relishing good food, and upholding her family's traditions. After she had kids, holidays seemed completely different. Managing even a few minutes of real conversation, grab-bing a single dinner roll to eat, or assembling a simple veggie tray was hard. While she had never had any problem eating three hours later than usual after waiting for a stubborn turkey to be cooked all the way through, now she had a tiny child whose tiny belly could last about three minutes before it needed another piece of cheese. She used to cherish her family's Christmas tradition of loafing in front of the TV watching A Christmas Story, *making guacamole, and scarfing tamales, but now her holiday was consumed with locating cheese that didn't have pepper jacks in it and preventing her toddler from eating Grandma's antique Hallmark ornaments, which really did look like real apples. Elaine realized that the different vibe of the holidays was consistently triggering a bad mood in her: she left feeling sad and frustrated that things weren't the same. After becoming aware of this, she started a new tradition of walking her kids and all their cousins to a nearby park and making a snowman with them on Christmas Day.*

TRY THIS

Identify one of the triggers that stirs up intense feelings in you. Is the trigger rooted in childhood or a passion or a fear? How could you handle your trigger in a new way?

49 Practice Nonattachment

Nonattachment refers to gracefully letting go of plans, expectations, and material goods. It involves mastering the skill of not holding things or events "too dear."

Here are a few things to avoid getting attached to:

Stuff: Maybe you once had a matching set of fancy glassware with swirly ridges. Over time, your kids broke all of them except for one exceptional survivor, and now you're mostly drinking out of old yogurt containers and Grateful Dead glasses with huge orange teddy bears on them that you got from the white elephant exchange. Your blue sweater never recovered after that time your baby, covered with beets, lunged at you from his high chair for an innocent hug. We need to wear old T-shirts, use super-cups left over from supersize meals, and smear chalk paint on our dining-room tables so kids can scribble all over it.

Meals: It's best to not get attached to plans for nice meals. Have frozen French toast for dinner, and eat lamb chops only when Grandma can make them. Maybe you used to be a decent cook, but since you had kids, you forget the timer for the noodles and take them out when they're still hard. The broccoli turns out so soggy you can't pick it up with a fork.

Plans: Don't set your heart on a concert, a party, or a cookie exchange. For the babysitter to show up as planned, all the kids to be free of stomach flu, and your cookies not to be burned would be the equivalent of winning the Powerball jackpot.

Vehicles: Let go of pride in your car, even if you used to be the kind of person who waxed it weekly. Maybe you planned never to let your kids eat or drink in the car, but then, on the thirteenth hour of a five-hour car trip, you broke down and handed over the entire box of crumbly graham crackers to your whining two-year-old. You put down a piddle pad to protect the car seat from a potty accident, but pee dripped on the carpet instead. It's best to see minivans as mobile snack shacks with built-in changing tables.

There are a lot of other things parents just can't hold too precious — like sleep, vacations, and flower beds. We can't get too attached to anything, or we will be miserable. The only thing we can really hold dear is each other.

Monkey Napkins

It was three days before the momentous first birthday party for Jackie and Seth's son, Nick. They had invited relatives over for a big bash and bought matching monkey plates, cups, and napkins. They had a monkey balloon and monkey goody bags — even a banana piñata. But the day before the party, Nick started coughing. When they took him to the doctor, he was tested for whooping cough (pertussis). "He can't have that — he was vaccinated for that," they protested. The next day, the doctor called to confirm that Nick had whooping cough and had to be quarantined for ten days. That gang of birthday monkeys seemed to mock them all afternoon. For the next week and a half Jackie and Seth stayed cooped up in their highly humidified apartment, wiping Nick's nose with monkey napkins and being grilled by the Centers for Disease Control. For their son's next birthday party, they focused less on the hoopla and more on him.

TRY THIS

Acknowledge an event, item, or way of relating that's been changed or destroyed. What was especially hard about losing it?

50 Back Off and Surrender

Your children are not your children.
They are the sons and daughters of Life's longing for itself.
They come through you but not from you,
and though they are with you yet they belong not to you.
— KAHLIL GIBRAN

You may want your child to play soccer, but he only loves to read. You may want her to wear the blue shirt, but she picks orange. You want him to eat asparagus, but the only veggie he'll touch is peas. It's incredible to watch children's personalities emerge, to see the people they're becoming, in all their blinding originality. However, it's not always easy to back off. We have a special role in children's lives as caretakers, boundary setters, guides, teachers, and the people who love them the most, but we don't control them.

Sock Dispenser

On his birthday, Shayna and Matt gave their son Jamal a train holder with perfectly sized compartments to store his collection of little train engines. Jamal refused to put a single train in it and instead called it his "sock dispenser." Every laundry day, he put a rolled-up pair of clean socks in each train compartment, and he fished them out each morning when he got dressed.

Let go of expectations that kids will turn out a specific way, do things how you dreamed they would, or follow in your footsteps. Be especially gentle with your feelings of loss around the way you thought your child would be (for example, expecting that you and your daughter would go to movies together) compared with what actually occurs (she hates movies). Let yourself be sad for what isn't, because doing so will free up energy to embrace what is, including the unique characteristics of the child in front of you.

Loving the Kid You've Got

Anthony had been an athlete all his life. He played three varsity sports in high school and played baseball in college. His son Daniel, eleven years old, was overweight and hated sports. On weekends, Daniel rode his bike to garage sales looking for old vinyl records to add to his impressive collection. He blasted music from way before his era, like the Beatles, on the bus ride to school and was mercilessly bullied by hordes of neighborhood kids. Daniel's dad had to work through his fear that his son would never really fit in, intense disappointment that he couldn't bond with his son through sports, and the unsettling feeling that his son's preferences did not resemble the ones he had dreamed of for him. He worked through his feelings so that he could love Daniel just as he was. If this meant looking through multiple secondhand stores to locate a sought-after bootleg version of Abbey Road *for Daniel's birthday, so be it.*

Another hard part of learning to let go comes when things don't go well between your kid and the outside world — whether school, sports, activities, or friends.

Toddler Classes

Tanya was a scrappy, elite soccer player when she was younger. She daydreamed about being her son's coach and practiced with him as soon as he could walk. Now here she was with her four-year-old for his park-district soccer debut. All the tiny kids stood on the blue line, trapping the ball with their perfect little Spider-Man shoes, just like the coach told them to — except hers. He was hiding in the corner of the goal with the netting over his head like a dead fish. She started to sweat. She pulled her tyke from the goal-net tangle. "Listen to the coach," she whispered through her teeth. Then she took a deep breath, got a drink from the drinking fountain, and decided, in that moment, to let go. As it turned out, she had to keep letting go for several more years: he never got good at soccer.

TRY THIS

Think of one thing you believe is important for your child to participate or excel in. How would you react if your child wanted nothing to do with it?

51 Let Go of Expectations

Expectations were like fine pottery. The harder you held them, the more likely they were to crack. — BRANDON SANDERSON

Let go of expectations. As a friend likes to say, "Happiness is having no preference." If you are not tied to things turning out a certain way, then you won't be upset when they don't.

Birth Plan Revisited

When Sadie was pregnant, she wrote an elaborate birth plan. She wanted to try to give birth naturally, without drugs, with her chosen music playing in the background, smelling lavender oil being rubbed into her shoulders as a crisp breeze blew through an open window. Her kind obstetrician smiled when she handed her the typed-out, super-detailed document.

Of course, not one thing on her long list came to pass.

Her baby came a month early, after her water broke suddenly. Instead of following her master plan, she endured thirty-six hours of labor, with enough Pitocin to induce labor in an elephant, and with not one but two shots of epidural anesthetics. She had planned on bouncing on a giant ball and using her special breathing technique to get through the contractions, but she was literally strapped to the bed as Edie Brickell's album Shooting Rubber Bands at the Stars, *from the 1980s, played in a loop for six hours straight. Her meditative state was disrupted when the dozens of cables she was hooked up to tangled into the kinds of knots that would stump an Eagle Scout. She planned to breastfeed right away, but her baby was too tiny, so she pumped milk for a full month before she could start nursing. She had planned to cuddle with her baby after birth, but he was whisked away to the NICU because of his low blood sugar, and she was so exhausted after not eating or sleeping for thirty-six hours that she passed out. When she later held her precious baby, Sadie wished she had been more focused on staying in the moment than on trying to control everything.*

Well-oiled routines may get colossally screwed up when the weather is below zero for twenty days in a row, your work schedule gets changed, or your great-aunt stays at your house for a few months. Your toddler, who always naps after lunch, may fall asleep in the car at ten in the morning because of a sudden growth spurt. Your son, who never cried at preschool, may start to wail after getting a bad sinus infection. Your baby may refuse to touch finger foods for two whole weeks as her canine teeth poke through.

Vacations can be especially frustrating if you've been looking forward to them and formed strong expectations of how they should go. On vacations with young children, let go of expectations and set intentions like these:

May this vacation be fun, a bonding experience, and a true
   adventure.
May this vacation result in lasting memories.
May I not be fazed by a thing.
May I remain playful, no matter what.

Accept that you may not get to rest, read a magazine, or watch
a ridiculously good old movie on cable from your hotel bed.

The following may also happen:

Kids may miss out on something amazing you'd planned
   for them because they fall asleep in the car on the way
   and are too drowsy or grumpy to enjoy it.
Kids may refuse to eat a fancy meal at a restaurant because
   it's got a "weird sauce."
No matter how short your vacation, at least one kid may
   come down with strep, impetigo, or an ingrown toenail while you're away.

TRY THIS

Think of one event that did not turn out remotely the
way you wanted it to. Imagine yourself loosening your
attachment to that activity in the future.

Embrace the Quiet, the Slow, and the Simple

52 Make Peace with First Gear

There is more to life than increasing its speed.
— MOHANDAS K. GANDHI

Research suggests that 28 percent of American people "always feel rushed," 45 percent report having "no excess time" (Robinson, 2013), and many see exhaustion as a status symbol (Brown, cited in Tippett, 2015). You may have been living a life in top gear for quite some time. You run to the train, speed down the road, and scarf lunch at your desk. Some days you just want to get to the park with your toddler for a quick romp, and it can be hard to slow down enough to enjoy her and her fantastic sense of wonder. She throws helicopter leaves twenty times, sits on every little ledge that looks remotely like a bench, squats down to see bugs and spider-webs, high-fives her shadow, picks up garbage to see what it feels like, jumps on leaves to crunch them good, and points out all the garden hoses.

Learn to value process just as much as content. Treasure the walk to the park just as much as the time at the park. Understand that preparing for a birthday party (putting up decorations, writing invitations, and making cupcakes) is often just as much fun for kids as the actual celebration. Note that things you do with kids to attend a travel baseball game (like jamming out on the car ride, having good conversations on the way, and stopping for ice cream on the way home) can be just as important for your relationship as being there to watch the game.

Kids are often rushed. To de-stress and preserve their mental health, they need time to dig in the sandbox, blow dandelions, add to a pinecone collection, and ride their tricycles. A survey of 1,500 children ages 5 to 11 found that children enjoy "simple pleasures," free play, and outdoor play more than organized trips. Their preferred activities included playing in the park or garden, making mud pies, playing in a kiddie pool, feeding ducks, climbing trees, and flying kites. They ranked organized trips much lower (Hall, 2012).

Boredom is also good for kids. It has the potential to foster creativity, motivation, and a more active pursuit of enjoyment and meaning (Knapton, 2015). If you've always been an overachiever, having a child may teach you to sink your teeth into the quiet space. Dance with a one-year-old who is spontaneously swaying to music. Blow bubbles and pop them. Learn to appreciate sipping a drink, drawing with a stick in mud, or taking a catnap.

When you're doing the 24/7 job of raising kids, identify specific things that help you or your child(ren) tend to energy in different ways, such as:

- a way to ground live-wire or anxious energy (such as deep breathing, gardening, or a salt bath)

- a way to boost energy (maybe a morning run, a favorite song, or a tall glass of water)
- a way to burn off excess energy (play soccer in the yard or have a dance party)
- a way to clear anger energy (expressing feelings, spending time in nature, or attending a counseling session)
- a way to build up energy reserves (such as eating more protein or going to bed an hour earlier for a week or two)

In addition, notice things that drain your energy:

- an energy leak (such as an inefficient system or bad habit)
- a complete energy wipeout (such as the flu or grief)
- an experience that saps your energy (like being in large crowds or airports)
- an experience that creates an adrenaline spike and crash (such as going to court regarding a custody issue)

Rest and relaxation are vital to preserving energy and well-being. Here are a few ways to prioritize downtime:

Snuggle on the couch or in bed with kids first thing in the morning. Be quiet together, read, or talk about plans for the day.

Resist signing your child up for every class. While it may seem important to teach kids robotics, French, or violin at an early age, signing up for only a few things at a time protects kids' opportunities for spontaneous play.

Enjoy free time outside every day. Play at the park, on the street, in the forest, or in the yard.

Color a picture with or beside your child.

Plan a restful vacation, maybe at a rustic cabin where kids can fish, play in the woods, ride bikes, or play board games instead of waiting in long lines for an amusement-park roller coaster or go-kart.

Practice one-tasking. Parents multitask so often that one-tasking — keeping your attention on one thing only for a period of time — can be restorative. For example, eat at least one meal per day without reading anything, scrolling on an electronic device, watching TV, walking around, or driving.

Have quiet time or an early bedtime. Give kids the opportunity to read, daydream, or snuggle with a stuffed animal before they pass out.

When your Facebook friends post photos of their families at a fancy dolls' tea shop or play-off hockey game, it's easy to feel pressured to take your kids to special events too. Work toward becoming 100 percent okay with playing in the yard instead. Let go of the belief that *going* somewhere special will *be* something special. Most kids are just as happy planting zucchini seeds as they are at fancy zoos.

People often equate being busy with being accomplished. What about the shadow side of busy? What if busy also means rushing out the door so fast that you miss a hug, forgetting to play music for weeks on end, or not having the time to call your best friend back? Imagine if, the next time someone asks how you are, you can respond with "Well-rested!" or "Terrifically balanced!" or "Never too busy to get together with you!"

If you allow an extra twenty minutes in the morning (maybe by getting up earlier), you can listen to a song, read your toddler a book, sip your coffee, or play with your baby's toes before rushing out the door. If you allow an extra twenty minutes at bedtime, you might spend five minutes being calm while your child begs to splash in the bathtub a bit longer, five minutes making up a silly game about teeth brushing, and five minutes laughing with your child about the day's events. You would still have five minutes left over to sing a lullaby or tell them a special story about when they were little.

If you allow an extra twenty minutes to get ready to leave for school and work, you can skip, tiptoe, and twirl with kids instead of herding and hustling them. Arriving at school or day care a little early also allows your child to warm up before the action starts.

It's easy to pack too much into a day and then get annoyed when children can't keep up the pace. Too many house projects, gymnastics drills, and piano lessons leave us wilted or high-strung. Taking children to Target, the park, and their cousin's school play in a single morning invites power struggles and ape-like behaviors. The slower you go and the fewer transitions you have, the more you can enjoy time with your children.

Spinning Strawberries

Theo and Connie were relieved to sit down to dinner and take the first gulps of their well-deserved beers. They had taken their kids to the carnival. All the lines, that high-pitched carousel music, squeezing into too-small spinning strawberries that made them want to hurl, and saying no to the too-scary rides and the expensive games and the funnel cakes had worn them out. But now their five-year-old, Zara, who was usually quite well-behaved at restaurants, was acting nuts. She made faces at the patrons on the other side of the booth, grabbed the knife out of the silverware bundle and swung it around like a pirate sword, and grabbed at everyone's French fries, even Grandpa's. Theo got fed up.

He eventually yelled and took away Zara's TV privileges for the next day. "We took you to a carnival all day, gave you treats, and now you act like this? What gives?" he thought. After tucking Zara into bed that night, Connie and Theo realized she had probably been overstimulated and overtired by the time they went out to eat. They had pushed her too far, and her behavior was not naughtiness but a result of being fried from the day's festivities.

TRY THIS

List the positive and negative connotations that slowing down has for you.

53 Be Playful

Follow the giggles. — LAWRENCE COHEN

Give yourself permission to play every day. Playful interactions create a climate for developing deeper, more intimate connections and help you stockpile resilience and vitality. The National Institute for Play describes play as "a refreshing oxygenating action whose hallmarks include humor, the enjoyment of novelty, the capacity to share a lighthearted sense of the world's ironies, the enjoyment of mutual storytelling, and the capacity to openly divulge imagination and fantasies" (National Institute for Play, n.d.). The author, researcher, and psychiatrist Stuart Brown defines play as engaging in a needless activity that's fun and pleasurable, whether it's tennis, dog walking, clowning around with a Whoopee cushion, or belting out songs (cited in Tartakovsky, n.d.).

Play is also children's most powerful means of learning, growing, and interacting. It can be inventive and hilarious. See where the day takes you — to a dance party, a hula-hoop contest, or a pretend restaurant that sells woodchip shakes and stick soup — even if you're not always sure it's a place you want to go. Sometimes it's a bit trying to enter a world of pretend pirates that live in forts made from eight of your freshly washed sheets. Sometimes you're not in the mood to play pig's puppet show or action supersquad. Overcome your reservations and get down on the floor with kids. Join in what they're doing, or creatively add to the scenario without taking over. To overcome your natural adult tendency to control things, try being silent, like a mime, while using exaggerated facial expressions to channel playfulness and connect with children who are just learning language. Lawrence Cohen, the author of *Playful Parenting* (2002), also advocates making time for physical play, such as roughhousing, playful wrestling, dog rides, and foot rides.

Here are some ways parents have found to be playful:

Hop on Pop: Whenever Yazan got home from work, he said to his kids, "Whatever you do, don't hop on Pop!" and this was the signal for them to jump on top of him and play-wrestle.

Race plopping on the beach: Dominique went for a walk on the beach with her son Joaquin. They started racing sprints and then stopping abruptly and flopping full-length into the sand. They also had fun making up other ways to race — backward, hopping on one foot, waddling, and crawling.

Knock-knock jokes: Kids laugh the hardest at their own jokes such as, "Knock, knock!" "Who's there?" "Sock." "Sock who?" "Sock toaster car seat mirror boo!"

Silly books: Use books that invite you to indulge in dramatic or silly reactions. Try *Yummy Yucky*, where you pretend to be grossed out by yucky things (saying, "Spit out!" and "Gross!"); *Rattletrap Car*, where you act flabbergasted by the car's falling apart ("Oh man, do you believe this?"); *The Monster at the End of This Book*, where you act scared of turning the page; *The Book with No Pictures*, which instructs the reader to say ridiculous things; or the Berenstain Bears books, where Papa messes up in all sorts of entertaining ways. One dad, Harrison, pretended to be really frightened of the ghosts and skeletons in Halloween books. His kids loved it when he shouted, "Yikes!" and buried his head under a pillow.

Punch bug — no returns! Play a passionate, playful game where you scream "Punch bug!" every time you see a Volkswagen Beetle car, as a way to have fun and help kids master the art of friendly competition.

April Fools: Help kids play April Fools' jokes, like having your six-year-old write a fake letter: "Dear Mom, you won ten million dollars and a free trip to Jamaica! April Fools!" or squirting ketchup on a kid's arm and acting like it's bleeding.

Crocodile hunter: At the park, let your kids capture you and throw you in an imaginary cage under the slide. Try to escape and have them run after you and catch you again.

Baby games: Use finger play and interactive baby games such as peekaboo, This Little Piggy (reciting the classic rhyme while wiggling each of baby's toes), or Roll, Roll Sugar Baby (singing, "Roll, roll, sugar baby, roll, roll, sugar baby" accompanied by actions like twirling arms, pushing arms out and pulling them back in, and clapping hands).

Silly Santa

As Lara drove her kids to school, she noticed a plastic Santa Claus still waving hello from a lawn in late January. Each school day, she and her children took bets on whether Santa would still be on the street. They did this until the third week of March, when Santa finally disappeared. Lara took her kids out for red sprinkle bakery cookies to celebrate Santa's finally being able to take a nap in the crawl space until the next holiday.

Let yourself enjoy the laughter and fun children bring, like when your daughter eats a vanilla yogurt and ends up looking like a polar bear; when she whispers during a christening, "Mom, when's the police [priest] going to pour water on the baby?"; or when she tells you, "Mom, the fire marshmallow [marshal] is coming to my school tomorrow!" Let yourself sometimes be the one who brings the fun like suggesting, "Let's all hide and jump out at Mom when she gets home from work!" or "Let's play restaurant for breakfast this morning! Who wants to be the waiter?"

TRY THIS

Name one of your favorite ways to be playful with your child.

54 Simplify

Our life is frittered away by detail.... Simplify, simplify.
— Henry David Thoreau

Many parents suffer from the frenetic subtype of burnout that is characterized by being overinvolved, overambitious, and overloaded (Montero-Marin et al., 2011). Focus on your highest priorities and cut out fillers. Be consistent and routine. Kim John Payne, the author of *Simplicity Parenting*, argues that children experience a "cumulative stress reaction" from too much enrichment, activity, choice, and toys. He asserts that children need serious "downtime" to balance out "up time." Payne conducted a study in which he simplified the lives of children with attention deficit disorder. Within four months, 68 percent went from being "clinically dysfunctional" to "clinically functional," and these children also displayed a 37 percent increase in academic and cognitive aptitude (Payne, 2010).

Here are some ways to simplify family life:

Bedtimes: Play calming music and speak quietly. Post the routine on the wall with pictures. Do things in the same order every night and read the same number of stories each night.

Travel: Pack snacks and lunches ahead of time. Stay in the same place for the whole vacation. Have low expectations for what you will accomplish. Have a plan B for bad weather.

Meals: Serve everyone the same thing. If they don't like the meal, they can always have Cheerios. Keep kids in high chairs until age 3. Serve healthy food most of the time. Let kids choose what and how much they want to eat.

Holidays: Celebrate holidays in the morning. Limit sugar by allowing kids one special treat, such as a cupcake. At parties, bring your own food for babies and toddlers. Leave even earlier than you intend to leave.

Toys: Rotate toys to avoid huge messes, overwhelm, and overstimulation. Keep some toys stored in the closet or the basement. Bring out only one toy with a jillion pieces (such as Legos) at a time.

Connections with your partner: Pick the same night of the week for date night for every week of the year. Use a shared calendar. Talk on Sunday night about plans for the rest of the week.

Birthday parties: Keep it small. Serve only three things. Host parties in the morning and keep crafts simple.

Sports and activities: Enroll children in a limited number of activities or hours of activities at a time. Stick to the limit. Research suggests that hours children spend doing organized sports are negatively related to creativity in adulthood, whereas time spent in unstructured sports is positively related to adult creativity (Bowers et al., 2014).

Eating out: Stick to restaurants that bring the food out fast. For dinner, go early, at 4:30 or 5:00, to beat the rush.

Playdates: Keep playdates to two hours. Serve a snack, and play outside if possible.

Simple Life

Petra drives an hour to an amusement park in the hot sun so that her four-year-old daughter Natasha can ride a kiddie roller coaster, go on the merry-go-round, and see Mickey Mouse. Natasha has fun, but the day is dampened by the stress of traffic, heat, long lines, expensive tickets, and sore feet. There are few moments to talk, play, relax, or bond. In Natasha's view, her mother is "the one who took me there." Next time Petra and Natasha go out, they visit a shady park close to home. They play store with pinecones and berries, swing on the swings together, and play hide-and-seek in the giant trees. In Natasha's view, her mother is "the one I had fun with."

TRY THIS

Think of one way you could simplify your family's life.

55 Use Your Phone and Facebook Strategically

With a beeping, jiggling, dinging device glued to your fingertips, it can be hard to throw a football around or give a high-five. With the whole world calling out from your pocket, it can be hard to appreciate the people right in front of you. "Just click on me," a notification coaxes seductively. And what do you see? Someone selling an old armchair. Someone posting a new pot roast recipe. An invitation to play a highly addictive online game. All things you could do without. Then you see something great: a funny message from a dear friend you haven't talked to in fifteen years. It draws you in, and random reinforcement strikes again, spurring you to check Facebook way more times than you should. Like a gummed-up, stuttering conveyor belt, phone surfing inches you along. It slurps up minutes when you're waiting in the hardware store or idling in the school pickup line. That's a good thing, right? But, the problem is, at the end of the day you're a little numb and aloof, and you can't remember the day's exquisite colors quite the way you'd like to.

Some kinds of online information enrich you: they show you a political candidate in a new light, a novel way to use vinegar, or a brilliant way to save for retirement. Others reveal your scientifically formulated porn-star name and compare your knowledge of Old World English to everyone else's knowledge of Old World English. Do you really, in all your human predictability, want to succumb to reading "Six Ways to Spot a Narcissist," "You'll Never Believe What Happened to These Conjoined Twins at Birth," or "What Your Fingernail Shape Says about Your Personality"? The minutes you spend on this kind of clickbait are minutes you will never, ever get back. Social media is so subtle, so sneaky about the way it stands in the room with you, calling out to you in a raspy voice, darkening your sunny outlook without your even noticing.

You may open up Facebook to read something like, "Look! Here's a video of little Johnny pedaling his bike with no training wheels at age 2!" or "Hooray for Anna, she learned how to swim by eighteen months old!" And you might think, "Oh no! My kid is four, and he still can't ride a bike without training wheels! Maybe I should get on that." Or "My two-year-old won't even put her neck in the water. I must be falling behind. Maybe I should sign her up for that very spectacular, very expensive swimming school." Or you might see photos from Joe and Sue, who are vacationing in the south of France while the grandparents watch their kids, and think, "Hey, I haven't even left my suburb since I had my baby."

A Facebook photo can do it to you. The Waltons are holding up bushels from an afternoon of picking berries, but you can't even get to the grocery store that day. The Smiths are goofing off with Tigger at Disney World, and you haven't had a vacation in two years. There's that video of Cindy the neighbor girl reading a chapter book aloud, even though she's not in preschool yet.

Whether it's through Facebook or some other means, every parent sometimes learns something amazing about another family or kid that can make them feel genuinely happy for the other people but a little bad about themselves. That experience may trigger very human feelings of doubt, guilt, panic, envy, or distress. You see the happy, carefree moments and conclude that these people must be perfect parents who have their act together, but you don't see their everyday challenges. You get a skewed, one-sided view.

Saltine Crackers

Nora liked to think about a family photo she posted on Facebook. "Love that new Facebook photo of your family!" a friend commented. "You all look so happy!" "That's funny," she thought. That photo was taken when they all had the stomach flu. They tickled the kids a little, just enough to make them smile but not puke again. The kids were squeaky clean because they had had the vomit rinsed off their hair in the bathtub. The kids' cheeks were flushed not from playing outside, but from fevers. They finally sat in one place all together because they were just too tired to move. Their parents looked fit, but really they'd just lost weight from a whole week on a diet of saltine crackers and flat 7-Up.

That was one of the hardest days of their entire lives, yet somehow it looked to the world like a perfect-family portrait and one of Facebook's notorious other-people-are-so-awesome reminders. How did that happen?

Bringing awareness to the way you interact with the behemoth social media empire, especially Facebook, can help you protect yourself from its negative effects. Consider the following:

Understand how Facebook affects your mood and outlook. Research suggests that the frequent use of Facebook "undermines well-being," increases envy (Verduyn et al., 2015), and makes people feel lonelier or worse about themselves (Steers, Wickham, and Acitelli, 2014; De Vries and Kuhne, 2015). In one study, the more the participants used Facebook over a two-week period, the more their life satisfaction levels declined (Kross et al., 2013).

Notice how Facebook fragments your day. Acquisti and Peer found that frequent interruptions make you 20 percent dumber — that is, you can recall information 20 percent less accurately when you've been interrupted while trying to remember it (cited in Sullivan and Thompson, 2013). Use an app (like Checky or Moment) to reflect on the number of times you check your phone and the total amount of time you spend on your phone.

Don't just look — post and comment as well. Direct interaction on Facebook — posting, commenting, and liking — is associated with greater feelings of bonding and social capital. However, passively consuming content is linked with increased loneliness (Burke, Marlow, and Lento, 2010) and "affective declines in well-being over time" (Verduyn et al., 2015).

Declutter your Facebook feed. Reconfigure the information you see from friends, acquaintances, and business pages so you read only what you want to read.

Evaluate how much Facebook intrudes on activities. Facebook use can whittle away at the pleasure derived from important real-life activities, such as eating dinner as a family, calling a friend, daydreaming, acknowledging a child, being intimate, and getting a good night's sleep. The intensity of the blue-wavelength light emitted by smartphone and tablet screens can disrupt our natural circadian rhythms and lower levels of melatonin (a factor linked to depression) (Moore, 2014).

Go on a Facebook diet or fast. One study found that 51 percent of parents log on to Facebook several times per day (Duggan et al., 2015). If you are overusing social media, delete apps from your phone, keep your phone out of your bedroom, or change to silent ringtones and alerts. Taking a break might alert you to the functions social media serves. You may find that you use it to distract yourself from a boring or difficult task, get a hit of dopamine from a brief connection, or brighten up dull moments.

TRY THIS

Use social media in a positive way, to spread as much kindness as possible for a day or a week. Post as many nice (and genuine) compliments as you can; use Messenger to check in with long-lost friends; send a sweet phrase to your partner or best friend; share quotes about kindness and love; share good memories about loved ones or publicly acknowledge them; or thank someone for sharing something that inspired you, taught you something, or made you smile.

Build Joyful Relationships with Children

56 Bond with Sweetness and Warmth

Every child needs at least one adult who is irrationally crazy about him or her. — URIE BRONFENBRENNER

Sensitive caregiving in the first three years of life is a strong predictor of an individual's social competence and academic achievement, not only during childhood and adolescence but all the way through to adulthood (Science Daily, 2014). It's easy to focus on children's behavior, academic performance, experiences, or skills instead of relationships. Notice what you talk about most: Is it your kids' feeding, sleep training, or a fancy new discipline system? Or is it how you enjoyed time with your child? When you're investing effort in a potty-training method, homework routine, or behavior system, ask yourself, "Does this strengthen my relationship with my child?"

Also consider extra steps you can take to be especially warm with your children, such as surprising them with a craft, a smiley-face pancake, or a walk around the block. Let your children know that you notice them, with phrases such as:

> "I saw how you let your sister borrow your special toy drill."
> "I saw you jump off the diving board today."
> "You were especially quiet when you woke up this morning."

Bring tenderness when your child is having a hard time, with phrases such as:

> "It looks like you need a cuddle. I'll give you a hug. Would you like to read a book or just sit on the couch?"
> "It looks like you're done and ready to go do something new. Would you like to ride your Big Wheel?"
> "Your friend had to leave, and you were having fun playing with him. You are real sad about that. Is that right?"

Leave your child thoughtful love notes with phrases such as:

> "I love you to Pluto and back."
> "I can't wait to go biking with you this weekend!"
> "Remember when you hit those tennis balls? I loved watching you!"

TRY THIS

Think about the family or environment you grew up in. What elements of it did you experience as especially sweet or warm?

57 Be Fully Present

Act as if what you do makes a difference. It does.
— WILLIAM JAMES

Being present to another person — including observing, smiling, enjoying, cuddling, acknowledging, discussing, doing something together, or commenting — is one of the highest forms of love.

Here are some ways to be fully present with children:

Say "I see you": We all need to be noticed and acknowledged. Use one-sentence narration, such as, "I see you cleaned up your toys," or "I see you are trying to get that knot undone," or "I see you riding your bike through the leaves!"

Ask permission to join: Ask your child, "Can I play blocks with you?" and build beside them. Ask, "Can I color with you?" and color beside them. Ask, "I see you're looking for shells. Mind if I join you?"

Eye contact: Look into children's eyes. Communicate empathy, curiosity, pride, and happiness through your gaze. Every time your eyes connect with their eyes, you build a little trust.

Use your child's name a lot, and with tenderness: The way you use your child's name, (with kindness, warmth, and love, or with annoyance, anger, and frustration), leaves an energy imprint on their name. Your child will begin to associate the tone you use with their sense of self.

Sit on your hands and bite your tongue: Be nearby and show support silently for a child's activities. Don't offer advice, butt in, take over, or teach. Don't shake rattles in your child's face, fill every minute with "educational activities," or "show" her how to play. Be present without judging, interrupting, correcting, adding, or suggesting.

Use touch: Hold your baby in your lap, carry him or her, cuddle, high-five, play-wrestle, and hug him or her.

Process hard moments with kids: Rather than always shielding kids from disappointments, hard moments, or flops, be present and kind as kids process them (and build resilience) (Brown, cited in Tippett, 2015).

Avoid interrupting and distracting kids with your own agenda: Preschool teacher Tom Hobson (Teacher Tom) writes, "A child is playing with marbles, exploring gravity, motion and momentum.

An adult picks up a handful of marbles and asks, 'How many marbles do I have?'...These stupid questions take a child who is engaged in testing her world, which is her proper role, and turns her into a test taker, forced to answer other people's questions rather than pursue the answers to her own" (Hobson, 2015).

Share laughter: Kids remember funny moments longer than others. Joke, tease, sing, dance, and be silly.

A Present Routine

Giselle hated how the evening got away from her after she picked her son up from childcare. She looked forward to seeing him all day, but she felt she had to rush through dinner and bedtime to get him into bed on time. Giselle started a simple routine of walking around the block with her son, playing ball in the backyard, and blowing bubbles before going inside for dinner. It only took about thirty minutes, but both she and her son treasured this time.

TRY THIS

For one minute, free-write about the ways you feel you are most present to your child(ren). How do they respond to your efforts?

58 Remember That Tiny Things Matter

Nothing you do for children is ever wasted.
They seem not to notice us, hovering, averting our eyes,
and they seldom offer thanks, but what we do for them
is never wasted. — GARRISON KEILLOR

A mountain climber will tell you that it doesn't matter what peak you scale: what you remember is the moose you spot at sunrise or how you made someone laugh when their feet were covered with blisters. It doesn't make a difference whether you take kids to roller coasters or roller derbies: it matters how you hug them goodnight. While no person can be "on" 100 percent of the time, making an effort to approach even a few tiny interactions with intentional positivity can strengthen relationships with children.

Reflect on:

How you greet a child upon getting home: hug and smile, or get right to business?

The first thing you say to your child in the morning: "Morning, beautiful!" or "Did you go potty yet?"

The first thing you do with your child in the morning: read a book on the couch, snuggle in bed, let them help you make coffee, check the weather together, or rush around?

How you ask your child to get ready to go out the door: "Five minutes to takeoff, can you zoom to our rocket ship?" or "Get in the car already!"

The first thing you say when you pick your child up from school: "It's so good to see you! Can I see what you made?" or "Did you turn in your library book?"

What you do when your child is taking a bath: play coffee shop as kids pour you water in a cup to pretend-drink, or read your phone?

What you do during dinner: sit down and have a friendly conversation, or check your email?

How you respond when your child gets out of bed during the night: gently walk them back to bed after a hug, or act frustrated and put out?

How you read a story: ask questions and use silly voices, or adopt a get-it-over-with tone?

Even five minutes or less of loving connection can have enormously beneficial results, as it releases neurotransmitters in the brain that make both you and your child feel satisfied and connected.

Here are a few ways to connect with kids in five minutes or less:

Give your child a dog ride (riding on your back as you walk around on all fours), a foot ride, piggyback ride, or shoulder ride.

Do your child's hair in a special way — braids, pigtails, or another style.

Help your child arrange their books the way they want them.

Fix your child a fancy drink, something they wouldn't normally have, with a curly straw or an umbrella. Sit on your stoop and sip together.

Ask your child to teach you something they know, like how to work their remote-control car.

Watch a funny theme song, video, or sports song together on your phone or computer.

Make popcorn together with an air-popper machine or on the stove top.

Go for a walk, bike ride, or scooter ride around the block together.

Show your child the stuff in your wallet, and ask if they have ideas about anything else you could put in there.

Talk about the pictures in one of your magazines or newspapers.

Play catch or kick a ball around together.

Play dollhouse. Make up stories about who's inside.

Play cars together. Zoom them, make ramps for them, and push them through tunnels made of paper-towel rolls or old PVC pipes.

How 'bout These Shoes, Mom?

"Mom! Can we help you get ready for work?" Jane's kids take out all of her necklaces and bracelets to help her pick one out. "No, I don't like that one. That's not pretty. Here, try this one. How 'bout these shoes, Mom? Do you like this hat? Whoa, you look nice, Mom!" Jane cherishes the time with her kids when she's getting ready for work.

TRY THIS

Think of a tiny interaction that's a "low-hanging fruit" — a fun five-minute activity you could easily do with your child.

59 Use Touch

The benefits of touch for young children — sitting in your lap, snuggling, baby wearing, kangaroo care (skin-to-skin contact with premature or other babies), scooching close while reading books, holding a child who is hurt, and hugging goodnight — are clear. Touch releases the neurochemical oxytocin, making both parents and children feel good. It can also help regulate hormones, decrease parental stress, and improve cognitive and emotional development (Harmon, 2010). Small pats or hugs make positive words more powerful and make cooperation more likely. Touch also provides feelings of reward and safety, reinforces reciprocity, and soothes (Keltner, 2010a).

A fascinating study by the researcher Dacher Keltner found that people could guess with surprising accuracy from a one-second touch on the forearm what emotion the person touching them was trying to convey: gratitude, anger, love, fear, or compassion (Keltner, 2010b). Be mindful of the emotions you convey to children through touch. Communicate love, kindness, compassion, or calm. Aim for ten positive, gentle pats or hugs per day. That's ten positive messages you can give your children without even talking. Pretty awesome.

TRY THIS

Think about how each of your kids responds to cuddles, hugs, pats, lap sitting, and other forms of touch. Which ones do they seem to like most?

60 Spend Special One-on-One Time with Children

Spend one-on-one time with each child. Kids adore the attention, the fun, and the indulgence of having a parent all to themselves. What's not as obvious is just how meaningful it can be for parents. If you feel exhausted from dragging multiple kids to swimming lessons, refereeing arguments, and cleaning up spills, spending special time with just one child can put the zip back in your step and the magic back in the moment.

What makes special time special?

It's one-on-one. A child who is used to sharing you with a fussy newborn sister or a potty-training brother finally gets you, the most important person in their life, all to themselves.

It invites complete presence. Naming time as special makes it more likely that you will give each other your full attention. No texting, no checking scores, no distractions.

It's fun. Labeling special time as such subconsciously makes you and your child look forward to it. It will be different from everyday life.

Here are some ways to make special time even more special:

Give your child a job. Ask your child to vacuum the car at the car wash or be in charge of buttering the pancakes at a restaurant. Ask him to be the one to put clothes in the locker at the swimming pool. It doesn't matter what the job is. When you give a child a defined role, they feel useful and cooperate more.

Let your child make a choice. Ask your child if she wants to play T-ball or soccer at the park. Ask if he wants to bake a pie or brownies.

Have fun. The most important part of special time is having fun. Look into your child's eyes, tease gently, and goof off.

Make a plan. Before special time, make a list of three to five things you might do or look for. If you are going to the park, you might see the fountain, ride the carousel, and get a hot pretzel. Before you go to the hardware store, talk to your child about finding the paint, the saws, and the key-making counter.

Take photos or videos. Have your child be the photographer, or look at the pictures together when you get home. Print out photos and make a small scrapbook.

Make a related art project. If you're going to fly a kite with your child, help him make a kite with colored construction paper, scissors, and glue. If you brought your child to the car show, print out a picture of her favorite car and let her paint it. If you go to the pool, make a collage before you go of magazine pictures of kids playing in water.

Don't forget the gear. Kids love gear (novel tools or items they can use for a task or an outing). Give them a scrub brush to wash grapes or potatoes, gardening gloves to help you pull weeds, or a Dustbuster to help you clean the car.

Replay the experience afterward. If you visit the largest tower in your city, try building it out of blocks when you get home. If you take your child to the dollar store, play at dollar store using a toy cash register, fake dollars, and aisles of toys.

Talk about the experience. "Remember when we went fishing and you caught that big pile of stinky seaweed?" "Hey, I can't believe that guy at the farmers' market gave you that flower for free. Wasn't that cool? We should tell Grandma about it!"

Here are some ideas for special things to do during one-on-one time at home:

Fix-it crew: Every 1st or 15th of the month, do chores together like changing light bulbs, replacing batteries in toys, and making minor repairs to your house.

Packing: Let your child help you pack for work trips, vacations, or the beach. Draw little pictures of items to check off as they put them in a suitcase. Ask if they have an idea for a fun surprise to pack.

Special book bin: Keep a bin of favorite books or kids' magazines to read only during special time.

Special art projects: Let your child choose a craft from a book of projects to make with you during special time.

Baking and cooking: Let your child measure, pour, and stir the ingredients, peel things, or do other jobs in the kitchen.

Gardening: Let your child water the plants with a spray bottle, a watering can, or a garden hose.

Cleaning projects: Let your child help with a project such as cleaning out canned goods or the fridge. Ask, "Can you take all the cans out of the cabinet and put them on the table for me?" "Can you line up all the garage stuff with long handles, like mops, rakes, and brooms?" "Can you sort my necklaces in whatever way you think is best?"

Here are ideas for special time when you're out and about:

- Take your child with you to the store.
- Play soccer, tennis, or another sport, or fly a kite at the park.
- Go to a car show.
- Visit an elderly or sick relative or friend.
- Watch a minor-league or high school sports game.
- Go on a short train ride together — just a few stops — to a new park.
- Bring your child to pick out a present for a birthday party.
- Take a paddleboat, canoe, or water taxi ride.
- Go to the zoo, a carnival, museum, mall, library, beach, or nature center.
- Go mini-golfing or fishing together.
- Go for a short hike in a forest preserve.

Golf Cart

Rob took his five-year-old golfing. His son was thrilled to ride in the golf cart and was proud of his jobs: marking initials on each ball with a Sharpie, throwing the balls and handing the tees to Dad, and putting in the last shot.

TRY THIS

Think about spending one-on-one time with a parent or other important adult when you were young. What effect did it have on your relationship?

61 Create Traditions and Rituals

Every Friday night, one family rents G-rated movies from the library, makes popcorn, and coasts into the weekend in total relaxation. Another hands out hot chocolate and bacon to 5K runners on Thanksgiving morning. Whether it's playing football in the snow on New Year's Day, volunteering on Memorial Day, or camping out on Labor Day, a family tradition offers a natural framework for bonding. Research suggests that rituals also help children build emotional health and resilience and provide buffers against mental health issues (Compan, Moreno, and Pascual, 2001; Goleman, 1992). The family ritual of eating dinner together is correlated with improved psychological well-being in children and with positive family interactions (Fiese, Foley, and Spagnola, 2006).

Baseball and Pie

Jack took his daughter to a baseball game every year when she was a kid. Not the whole family of six — just him and her. They ate peanuts

*in the shell, shook hands with the furry mascot, joined in silly chants
and cheers, and people-watched. They stopped on the way home for a
slice of French silk pie. Twenty years later, they still catch a baseball
game together once a year and still stop for pie.*

TRY THIS

Think of a new family ritual that would offer a chance
for bonding and fit your family's interests.

62 Bond over Adversity

When you feel sucked into disciplining, fixing, or getting frustrated with kids' powerful emotions, resist. These trying moments can be great opportunities for bonding.

Here are a few situations that might provide unexpected bonding opportunities:

When kids are sick: If you think of caring for your child when he or she has a mild illness as a potential bonding experience, you might look forward to taking the day off work instead of dreading it. You can create a get-well box filled with kiddie magazines like *High Five* and *Ranger Rick* that can be read only when a child is sick. You might put in special art projects, new books, Gatorade, or a stuffed animal. You might make your child a homemade get-well card, play their favorite music, and watch their favorite movie. You can hold them gently if they're crying or coughing. After visiting the doctor, you can take them out for a slushy. Instead of feeling put out, you can enjoy comforting them in their time of need.

When kids are acting out: When children are acting out or breaking the rules, there is another opportunity to bond and deepen your connection. You can sit beside children, provide the time and space for them to settle, or talk quietly, in short phrases, at eye level. You can stay calm and firm and listen to their feelings without excusing their behavior. You can reconnect, give them a big hug. This response builds your children's trust that you will provide consistent boundaries to keep them safe.

When kids are tired: A tired child is a different child. Exhausted children whine, cry easily, lose their tempers, and don't cooperate. By bringing patience to interactions with a tired child, you can show them that whatever their mood, you will be there for them, unwavering in your compassion.

TRY THIS

Think about how your child behaves when overtired. How do you usually react?

63 Set Up Ways for Children to Use Their Strengths

Children see themselves reflected in the eyes of their parents. When they know their parents adore them, understand their strengths, and believe in them, they internalize that faith and start to believe in themselves. Notice when children light up with passion or self-confidence so you can create opportunities for them to do the things they love.

Here are a few examples:

Helping with babies: You may have a daughter who loves helping with babies. This puts her leadership energy and kindness to good use. When a friend comes over with a baby, help your daughter make a baby basket filled with soft baby toys, teethers, pacifiers, and a receiving blanket. Ask, "Could you sing a lullaby to the baby if she starts fussing? Which song do you think the baby would like today?"

Being playful: You may have a son with a great sense of humor. Prioritize funny activities like peekaboo, talking in wild voices, and silly teasing. Ask yourself, "Did I make enough time to be playful with him today?" Notice if he is more content when he has gotten his fill of joking around.

Running: You may have a son who loves to run. He wants to have races, play sports, play tag, and play chase. He needs time scheduled each day to go to sports class, kick the ball in the yard, and run around the house, just like the time scheduled for brushing teeth and baths. While gardening, give him the job of running across the yard to fetch a shovel, seeds, or a watering can. While packing, ask him to run around the house to fetch swimsuits, washcloths, or socks. When he gets a chance to run around, notice if he appears happier, sleeps better at night, and seems more regulated.

Coloring: Give a daughter who loves to color ample access to crayons, markers, and paper and let her draw and color without interruptions or suggestions. Send her drawings to a grandparent or a babysitter or post them on the fridge. Notice if coloring helps her wind down from school, wait patiently for dinner to be ready, and settle down before bedtime.

Packing Party

Rob had always been a giving child with a big heart — he collected the most pennies for the penny drive at school, made cards for his elderly grandma, and helped his mom, Carla, shop for coats and mittens for kids at the shelter. For his ninth birthday, Rob asked Carla if he could bring friends to a Feed My Starving Children packing site to assemble food packs for kids in other countries, just like he had done with his scout troop a few months prior. His mom agreed, and Rob and seven of his friends spent two hours packing food while listening to their favorite music, then had cupcakes outside. A few of the boys who attended the party commented to their parents that it was one of their favorite birth-day parties: they enjoyed helping others, too.

TRY THIS

Think of a positive trait that seems central to your child's identity. What's one way you could create space for your child to show and develop that trait?

64 Think and Speak of Your Child in Positive Terms

Use positive words to describe your child. Language has a huge impact on self-image and other people's expectations. When educators first meet a child who is described to them as "hyper," "crazy," or "out of control," they subconsciously look for confirmation of that behavior. However, when that same child is described as "spirited," "helpful," "an out-of-the-box thinker," "an artist," or "a solid, loyal friend," they are on the lookout for those gifts instead.

Two Hundred Stickers

Abby, a three-year-old, had unusual drive and focus. She did things in very particular ways. She might spend an hour putting every sticker from a two-hundred-sticker pack on a card for Grandma. If she did a thumbprint picture project at school, she made seventy thumbprints to cover every inch of a poster-size sheet of paper. If she played with Legos, she used every single one in the bin to make a tower. Outside, she played with her toys and Big Wheel in the same order every day. She made patterns out of everything.

At one point in her toddlerhood, Abby's mom, Deanna, worried that she might have aspects of obsessive-compulsive disorder (OCD). But when she mentioned this to Abby's pediatrician, the doctor replied, "My niece was like that as a child, and for a while I worried about the same thing. Then she grew up to be a chemical engineer!"

The pediatrician told Deanna that she thought it was sad that we often see any unusual behavior in kids as problems or disorders to be diagnosed. Kids' best strengths are the very things that often trip them up. It's the adults around them that expect them to conform to "normal" standards, like putting only ten stickers on a card.

The next time Deanna felt like Abby was ignoring her when she asked her to get ready to go to gymnastics class, she recalled her astounding gift of tuning out distractions. She started using different language to describe her. "Abby has incredible focus. She enjoys sinking her teeth into something. She craves a sense of order. She loves to master new things. She has a real gift for not just doing what's expected but going above and beyond."

TRY THIS

List five positive words you could use to describe your child.

65 Use Your Child's Strengths to Help Overcome Their Challenges

Sometimes focusing on children's strengths quite magically takes the power out of certain problems. Focusing on strengths can transform problems or be the very key to solving them.

Ghadir, a first grader, experienced extreme anxiety in the mornings before school. He loved music, so his teacher allowed him to listen to music with headphones while he waited in the hall for school to start. His anxiety decreased.

Ebony, a preschooler, resisted transitions and wouldn't go potty, put her socks and shoes on, or help load the car. She loved coloring, writing her letters, and having defined roles and jobs. Her mom helped her write out the day's scheduled activities and color in pictures of the activities. She gave her a clipboard and a clothespin and put Ebony in charge of telling the family what was next and moving the clothespin down the list as they completed each activity. Having this special job to do improved her cooperation.

Nathan had a hard time completing his second-grade homework at night. He was an early riser and full of energy in the morning, so his parents started helping him with homework before school instead.

Gabriel was disruptive in school assemblies. He was an oldest child and loved helping his younger brother and sister. When the school set up Gabriel to be a mentor and buddy for a younger child during assemblies, his behavior improved.

Rhena hated brushing her teeth. She loved Elmo. Her mom let her brush her stuffed Elmo's teeth before she brushed her own. The mom brought two Elmo books and asked Rhena to choose which one she wanted to read when she was finished brushing her teeth.

TRY THIS

Think of one behavior that you'd like to help your child improve on. List some of your child's key strengths or interests, and identify ways you could use their strengths to improve the behavior.

66   Offer Opportunities for Children to Help Others

Using data collected over twenty-five years, the researcher Marty Rossman found that children who had done chores since the age of three or four were likely to be better adjusted, have better relationships with friends and family, and be more successful in their careers (Dishongh, 2015). While kids can learn to do tasks for themselves, such as clear their plates or make their beds, it's also important for them to do jobs that help others. They are highly motivated by helping family members, friends, or even strangers. They love using their expertise and enjoy the ownership and independence that accompany their jobs.

Setting the Table

Tina will never forget the Christmas when she took her four-year-old son, Mark, to visit Santa, to the tree-lighting ceremony, and to Christmas story time at the library.

She and her husband chose the perfect present for their construction-loving kid — a toy workbench — and stuffed Mark's stocking with markers, Spider-Man toothbrushes, and glow sticks. They let him open each chocolate door of the Advent calendar, listen to Christmas music, read Christmas stories, and make a bunch of ornaments from scratch.

However, when Tina asked Mark what his favorite part of the holiday was, he answered, "Helping Grandma set the table for Christmas dinner."

When Tina looked back at the season, she could see that Mark lit up the most not on Santa's lap but when he helped Daddy shovel snow. His eyes shone most brightly not when he was tearing open a new building set but when he was carefully cutting paper or ripping tape to help her wrap presents, putting stamps on their holiday cards, baking cookies, watering the Christmas tree, and hanging lights on their bushes. She realized that letting Mark help with her tasks was the best gift she had given him.

Here are suggestions for everyday jobs little kids can do to help out:

- Get people a glass of water when they come over
- Open packages or boxes with kiddie scissors
- Put muffin cups in the muffin baking pans
- Match Tupperware lids with containers
- Sort silverware from the dishwasher basket
- Squirt ketchup on everyone's plates
- Push a vacuum cleaner
- Be the house DJ, choosing music and playing the songs
- Squirt water on tables and scrub them with a washcloth

- Dry off wet playground equipment with a towel at the park
- Check the weather forecast in the morning and tell everyone what it is
- Use tongs to serve everyone dinner food (like chicken pieces)
- Make party decorations
- Pass out snacks to siblings or friends
- Call grandparents, friends, or cousins to invite them over for visits

TRY THIS

Identify one job that each of your kids could do to help out the family.

67 Complete Good Deeds with Children

Setting children up to do good deeds helps them develop thoughtfulness and gives them experience helping others. Kids love the excitement and intrinsic reward of making a contribution.

Here are some good deeds to do with kids:

"We'll let that woman go through the checkout first — it looks like she really has to get somewhere."

"Let's do a good deed and get everyone something special from the grocery store. Dad will like pepperoni, your sister will like watermelon, and your brother will like fruit bars. They're gonna be so surprised!"

"You know what Grandma loves? Gluten-free bread. Let's buy some for her."

"We are doing a good deed today by shoveling snow off our walkway. Now all the people walking to the train won't slip when they go past our house. Let's shovel our neighbor's walk too, in case they don't get a chance to. Wouldn't that be a good deed?"

"Let's make a get-well card for your cousin, because she's not feeling well. Can you think of anything else that might cheer her up?"

"When our friends come over, we can make sure everyone has a toy they like, even the babies."

"You cleaned up the playroom while Mom was upstairs? That sure was a good deed."

"I know something we could do for a good deed today! Match all the socks. That would help our whole family."

"It looks like your brother dropped his mac and cheese. Would you like to do a good deed and give him a scoop of yours?"

"We're going to send Alana flowers at the hospital to help her feel better. Would you like to help me choose them?"

Showing children how to act with kindness can remind us to be more thoughtful ourselves.

TRY THIS

Think of a good deed you and your child could do for someone you know right now.

68 Listen for Messages Hidden in Children's Behavior

If you sat in a conference room with your eyes closed and listened to the speaker's words, you'd only catch about 10 percent of what's actually going on. If you went into the same room and paid attention to other things, you'd understand a lot more. From the speaker's body language, tone, and paraverbal communication, you would intuit the meaning behind the words: "Finish by the deadline!" "Teach to the test!" "Sell, sell, sell!" From interaction between the speaker and the audience, you'd sense the hidden agendas: vying for power, airing old baggage through subtle jabs, or trying to inspire.

Evolved listening goes beyond hearing words to comprehend complexities such as what speakers want you to understand, why it's important to them, and what they want you to do next — even if they don't say it outright. We can fine-tune our listening skills so that instead of just hearing words or seeing behaviors, we get the real message — and do something about it. This is just as true with children as with business executives.

Some children's behaviors and their potential underlying meanings:

Following you around, being your shadow, trying to push your computer buttons, grabbing the vacuum from you, dumping out the mail, or trying to open a package = "I want to help you."

Resisting routines, saying no, refusing the yellow plate or the green cup, not eating breakfast, or not cooperating with brushing teeth or putting pajamas on = "I want some power and control."

Dumping out or breaking toys, ignoring, fighting over, or playing aggressively with toys = "I need a break from toys. I want to go for a walk, make music, do art, go somewhere, or cuddle."

Rubbing eyes, slowing down, fussing, whining, and acting out = "I'm tired."

Throwing food on the floor, walking out of the room, and coloring on a wall = "I want some attention" or "I'm tired."

Sitting on your lap, hugging, snuggling, making you cards, being silly with you, and trying to help you = "I love you."

Lying around, acting crazy or out of character, zoning out, not eating, or not doing much = "I'm getting sick."

Not getting in the car seat, not putting shoes on, not packing a backpack, not going potty, and just lying on the couch = "I need some quiet time."

Punch

Brendan was chatting to his adult friends about his six-year-old son, Derek, when Derek was in the room. "Derek's not quite sure about

*riding a bike on his own, are you, Derek?" he said. "I asked him if he
wanted to try it, and he was scared he'd fall." Derek went up to his dad
and punched him on the arm. Later, Derek confided to his dad that he
was embarrassed to hear him talking about his fears in front of other
adults, and punched him to get him to stop.*

TRY THIS

Identify a challenging behavior that your child sometimes engages in. What do you suspect he is really trying to say by it?

69 Complete the Most Important Bedtime Ritual

A consistent bedtime routine helps children sleep better and longer (Staples, Bates, and Petersen, 2015) and can be a beautiful, powerful way to bond with children. Research suggests that bedtime routines are a form of "relational work" that helps children develop their capacity for "communion with others" (Sirota, 2006). They also reduce parenting stress, which in turn has a positive effect on children's emotions, behavioral regulation, and readiness to learn (Zajicek-Farber et al., 2014).

Lap sitting and cuddling during story time gives kids the touch they need. Hearing a story also helps kids learn new concepts, language, and prereading skills. Helping kids brush their teeth and put on their pajamas teaches independence and self-care. Getting children that last drink of water, fixing their blankets, and tucking them in reinforces your role as their nurturing caregiver. Telling kids you love them, that you're proud of them, and that you notice them reminds them that, despite any dramas, they will always be your favorite people.

The most important bedtime ritual of all is *listening*. Bedtime is a perfect, quiet time for kids to express themselves, talk about doubts or fears, tell you silly things that happened, and share their favorite parts of the day. Kids spend much of their days being talked to, but it's important to create opportunities for them to lead the conversations. It strengthens your relationship and creates a pattern that can persist into adulthood.

Of course, not all kids spontaneously open up. To encourage them, review the day's details and leave giant pauses to help them remember anything they want to tell you:

Sensory details: "Brrr, it sure was cold outside!" Or "We really got stuck in the gooey mud on that nature trail!"

Social details: "That was neat to have Ava over today. She really liked your baby doll, but you wanted her to play ponies with you."

Emotional details: "I was so surprised when Grandma stopped by! What fun to see her!"

Scratch

Cole and Savannah, a brother and sister only a year apart, had a rough day at the same summer camp. Cole had called Savannah stupid, and Savannah had scratched her brother on the neck. The teacher put them both in time-out. At bedtime, their mom listened as Cole told her the whole story. "I called Savannah 'stupid' because I was trying to play with a boy who I wanted to be friends with. Savannah knocked down his tower, and I thought he wouldn't want to be my friend anymore. I was really mad." Then the mom went into Savannah's room to listen to her description of what happened. "I wanted Cole to play with me, not with that boy. That's why I knocked down his tower." After listening to them both, she talked with both kids about what to do next time.

TRY THIS

Think of one change you could make to strengthen your child's bedtime routine.

70 Whisper

How you say things to kids — playfully, kindly, or in a whisper — is a cornerstone of your relationship with them. Whispering has been found to be associated with playfulness, tenderness, and bonding. If you whisper, it catches attention, it's special, and it's sweet. It also has a strong "contagious" effect, so it can be used to help children calm and quiet themselves (Cirillo, 2004).

Ms. Lee's Legacy

Ms. Lee, a first-grade teacher, was extremely soft-spoken. With her volume, that of a wee mouse, you had to lean in seriously close to hear her, and you often had to ask her to repeat things. Ms. Lee never raised her voice to her students, and amazingly, they cooperated and spoke in whispers too. Ms. Lee showed that if you are quiet, the kids around you will be quiet, too.

Here are six ways to use a whisper:

For cooperation: When your child won't put his socks and shoes on and you're running late, a whisper of "Socks and shoes" invites cooperation.

For love: At bedtime, whisper, "I love you" or "I'm so glad you are my daughter" into your child's ear.

For calm: When your child is getting hyped up or running a bit wild, ask, "Can I ask you something?" or "Can I tell you something?" Lean in and talk to them in the quietest possible voice. Whispering can help ground overzealous energy.

For cooperation: When you think of a way your child can help out, whisper, "I have a special job for you. I want you to do *X*. What do you think?"

For healing and reassurance: When your child skins a knee or stubs a toe, whisper, "I'm sorry you're hurting. I hope you feel better soon."

For excitement: Whisper to build enthusiasm when you're going somewhere special, like the swimming pool or a party.

TRY THIS

Rate your normal voice volume on a scale from 1 to 10 (with 10 being loudest).

71 Banter with Children

Banter, or informal and spontaneous chatting, gossiping, joking, and storytelling, is highly beneficial for young children. Research shows that 86 to 98 percent of the words used by a child by the age of three are derived from their parents' vocabularies. Daily exchanges between a parent and a child have been shown to expand children's knowledge and skills and have lasting effects on their performance later in life (Hart and Risley, 2003).

Some benefits of banter:

Creating a language-rich environment: Talking about your neighbors, weekend plans, the funny thing Grandpa said, the construction project across the street, phases of the moon, or a trip you once took all build your kid's vocabulary.

Fostering intellectual development: By talking about a curtain rod that's been difficult for you to fix, what you should do with your day now that it's raining, or what present you should buy for your great-aunt's ninetieth birthday, you invite children to help you solve problems. You can also encourage intelligent curiosity with questions like "I wonder what you'll have for your snack at school," or "What do you think Mom will pack for her hiking trip?"

Fostering sensory development: When you talk about sensory details such as the delicious smell of the banana bread in the oven, the sound of an airplane, or the sour taste of your grapefruit, kids become more in tune with their own senses.

Building resiliency: When you describe tough things that happened to you and how you dealt with them, you model ways for kids to solve their own problems. "I remember when I got a flat tire in the rain. I asked this woman to help me fix it, and she did. That was so nice of her."

Cultivating social skills: Showing a genuine interest in others and being able to listen and talk to people about anything is an essential social skill.

The best banter is a combination of asking questions, listening, laughing, and bringing up topics, but it's not always easy to carry on a conversation with a toddler. Here are some sample topics:

- what's going on in your neighborhood — the art fair, the construction of the new condo building
- your favorite place in the world to visit and why
- what you're most excited about right now
- what cousins, grandparents, or aunts and uncles are up to
- the changing seasons

- what you're grateful for today
- some things on your to-do list

TRY THIS

List some of the things you and your kids love to talk about.

72 Give Children Ownership and a Say

Giving kids a say in decisions builds respect, capitalizes on their normal developmental need for power and control, and invites cooperation. However, too many options and big decisions can overwhelm young children. They want and expect their parents to provide structure and make key family decisions, as it helps them feel safe.

Limit young children's choices to two alternatives. If they don't or can't pick between the two, don't offer a third. (This doesn't include free play, where they can do whatever they're interested in.)

Be consistent about the ways you give kids decision-making power. If one night you ask, "What do you want for dinner?" and the next night you say, "We're having tacos, and you can't have anything different," they are likely to feel frustrated and confused. If one weekend you ask, "What do you want to do this morning? We can do anything you want," and the next weekend you tell them, "Pack up, you're going with Dad to the grocery store," kids may not understand the inconsistency and may resist.

Shovel

Teresa was fed up with her son Ramone's books being scattered all over the floor each night. "How do you think we could keep your floor cleaner?" she asked.

"I think we should shovel them into a pile and then put them back on the shelf," Ramone replied.

Teresa said, "Okay," and got a small shovel for Ramone to keep in his room. She handed it to him each night before bed. "Wow," said Teresa a few days later, "this shovel idea you thought of is really working out. I can see the floor is as clear as ever!"

Here are some ways to give young children ownership and a say in decisions:

> Ask if they want to use a packaged thank-you card for their teacher or make their own.
>
> Ask if they want you to butter their pancake or butter it themselves.
>
> Ask if they want to listen to jazz or rock and roll.
>
> Ask if they want you to hang a photo in their room over here or over there.
>
> Ask if they want to play I Spy or listen to music while riding in the car.
>
> Ask if they want to watch TV before or after lunch.
>
> Ask which homework activity they want to complete first.
>
> Ask if they think you should buy dad a coffee cup or a football hat for his birthday.
>
> Ask if they want to wipe the table or sweep the floor.

Ask if they want their banana whole or cut into pieces.
Ask if they want to ride in the cart or walk in the grocery
store.

TRY THIS

Think of one problem that you could ask your child to
solve along with you.

73 Balance the Three Types of Play

It's important to provide kids with opportunities for the three main types of play: independent (solitary) play; adult-child interaction (for example, floortime and having kids assist with adult tasks); and social free play with other kids (including parallel or side-by-side play, social play, and cooperative play). Each has unique benefits.

Independent solo play in a safe space helps kids learn skills, solve problems, and self-regulate. Babies love playing with their toes, discovering the texture on their sleeves, and learning cause and effect from pushing a ball. Older children need quiet time to learn to amuse themselves, discover interests, collect their thoughts, and become self-directed.

To encourage independent play, set up a simple, safe play space. Also consider rotating open-play scenarios that include objects such as:

- acorns, sticks, bark, leaves, stones, and containers
- an old phone, computer keyboard, and desk

- wooden blocks
- a cash register and play food
- wrapping paper and cardboard boxes and tape
- king-size sheets, clothespins, and chairs
- paints, paintbrushes, and cups of water
- jewelry, high heels, bow ties, and fancy hats
- tube-shaped pasta and strings

Mix objects at times, and be open to discovering how children creatively combine toys in unique ways (like painting acorns or gluing tube-shaped pasta to decorate presents).

Balance independent play with adult-child play, which helps children develop strong bonds and build language and skills. The psychiatrist Stanley Greenspan used the term *floortime* to describe getting down on the floor with children, playing with them, and building on their strengths through warmth and interaction. While floortime was originally developed as an intervention for children with developmental delays or autism, it is appropriate for all children, at any age. Get down on the floor with kids and follow their interests, whether that means playing with blocks, a toy kitchen, trains, a sand tray, or a dollhouse. Play make-believe and tell stories. Make funny faces after drinking out of their toy teacups, or build castles with them out of Legos. Keep it fun, because if it is forced or becomes a power struggle, positive outcomes dwindle.

Greenspan identifies three key objectives of floortime:

- follow your child's lead — enter the child's world
- challenge her to be creative and spontaneous
- expand the interaction to include most of her senses and motor skills and different emotions ("Greenspan Floortime Approach," 2015)

While floortime is important, children also love being included in grown-up activities. They feel proud when helping to rake leaves, shop for groceries, or clean Mom's golf gear. Kids often love to partake in adult errands, work, and life activities, especially if they're given jobs or a role along the way. Make a ritual of always doing certain things together: always hang holiday lights with your daughter, or always ask your son to help you at the farmers' market.

Here are some ways to include kids in adult worlds:

Taking care of pets: Let kids help you feed, walk, play with, or clean up after a pet.

Going to the hardware store: Bring kids to the hardware store and let them measure rope, choose between two paint colors, or pick out a key ring.

Paying bills: Let kids put the return address stickers and stamps on envelopes and carry them to the mailbox.

Getting ready for a fancy event: Give your child an old lipstick or eyeliner to decorate a smiley face on a piece of paper while you put on makeup. Let your child try on jewelry, belts, jackets, or ties while you try on yours.

Watching sports: Let your child watch part of a game with you. Share popcorn and teach them about the game. Give them a scarf or flag to wave and make a sign to hold up. Wear team jerseys and bet on the score.

In addition to helping kids play solo and with adults, set up opportunities for kids to play with other kids, outside of recess or day care. Research suggests that social free play helps children learn how to make decisions, solve problems, exert self-control, follow rules, regulate emotions, make friends, and get along with others. Most importantly, it helps children relieve stress and experience more happiness (Gray, 2011; Barnett, 1984).

While many parents used to be able to send kids outside to play with neighborhood kids, it's rare to find whole groups of kids playing outside anymore, so parents often need to take an active role in setting up playdates or playgroups, or teaching older children to make arrangements on their own. As the writer Malcolm Harris says, "We live in an era of the playdate.... The idea of kids so busy they need adult secretaries to pencil in time with their friends is both silly and real" (Harris, 2016). Besides setting up play plans, the writer Esther Entin (2011) recommends that parents "begin to identify small changes — such as openings in the schedule, backing off from quite so many supervised activities, and possibly slightly less hovering on the playground — that would start the pendulum returning to the direction of free, imaginative, kid-directed play."

TRY THIS

Think about your kids' balance between the three types of play. Is there anything you would change?

74 Access the "Green Advantage"

When researchers compared the effects of completing indoor and outdoor activities on kids with attention-deficit hyperactivity disorder (ADHD), they found that outdoor settings resulted in greater reduction of ADHD symptoms, a factor they term the "green advantage" (Kuo and Taylor, 2004). Research also suggests that immersion in nature can help make people more caring, generous, and helpful (Weinstein, 2009; Gueguen and Stefan, 2016) and that exposure to green space may reduce depression, anxiety, and stress (Beyer et al., 2014). One meta-analysis of ten studies found that exposure to "green exercise," or "activity in the presence of nature," resulted in improvements in self-esteem and mood, with the benefits being even greater in settings with water (Barton and Pretty, 2010). A survey of mothers in sixteen countries found considerable agreement that playing outside, at playgrounds, or at parks was their children's most enjoyable activity (Singer et al., 2009). Time outdoors every day is one of the best gifts you can give children.

Park Intervention

Sandra noticed that her son seemed more down and lethargic after starting first grade. He had always been an outdoor kid, and now he got only twenty minutes of recess in a school day more than six hours long. Sandra decided to take him straight to the park for an hour after school each day. Within a week, she noticed a difference. He seemed to get some of his old energy back and asked to go biking on the weekend instead of saying he was too tired.

TRY THIS

Think of one easy way you could incorporate more outdoor time into your family's day.

75 Have Compassion for Children's Weak Spots

Even though we have our own weak spots, it can be very painful to learn of our children's. Addressing a child's significant special needs, health problems, or developmental issues may pose enormous challenges and require expert intervention and support, for both child and parents, that are beyond the scope of this book. Less serious conditions may also place practical and emotional demands on parents. We may grieve, going through the stages of denial, bargaining, anger, and sadness (not necessarily in that order) before accepting the situation. But learning to accept children's weak spots can call forth from us a deeper level of love, intuition, and wisdom.

A child's physical weak spot might be present at birth, such as a birth defect or lung problem. It may emerge later — a peanut allergy, a weak stomach, a sensory deficit, or a susceptibility to ear infections. A baby may have eczema or huge tonsils that interfere with sleep. One has trouble reading social cues, while another's legs are not fully formed. Certain weak spots may not reveal themselves until later in life, as a result of overuse or stress. Some weak spots run in ancestral chains (cultural, behavioral, or genetic), such as anxiety, shyness, stubbornness, sugar or alcohol addictions, or heart problems.

Children are born with emotional weak spots too, like being hypersensitive, quick to anger, easily distracted, or perfectionistic. Emotional weak spots and strengths are often two sides of the same coin. A child with a creative mind may fight back against rote schoolwork. A child who has a strong will may be a good leader but resist limits. A child with incredible focus may have trouble transitioning between activities. A child who is in tune with everyone's feelings may experience emotional highs and lows from picking up on those feelings.

Weak spots demand that we muster strength, ask for and receive support, and interact in even better ways. We learn to enjoy and love children not just when they are "good" or "easy" but also when things are hard.

Sunscreen

Joshua's weak spot, a sensory integration issue that made him hate having anything on his skin, challenged his mother to rise to the occasion while applying sunscreen before they went outside. Instead of just slathering on the sunscreen, she needed to be patient and calm, joke with him to take his mind off the process, and ask him what he felt could make it go better. She also found she needed to ground herself before she began applying sunscreen and let go of the stress she felt when he engaged in surprising antics to avoid it. His weak spot spurred her personal growth.

Hearing

Sonya failed the preschool hearing screening because of fluid in her ears. While the doctor weighed the pros and cons of inserting ear tubes,

Sonya's parents had to evaluate the way they talked to their daughter, whose hearing was somewhat impaired. Instead of simply saying things more loudly when she did not respond, they learned to move closer to her and speak more gently and patiently. Sonya's weak spot challenged them to strengthen their communication skills.

TRY THIS

Think of one way that your child's weak spot propels your personal growth.

76 Understand the Factors That Contribute to Children's Behavior

Understanding factors that feed into children's behavior helps us address it with more kindness and patience. Factors that contribute to children's behavior often include the following:

Core conditions: When children act out, melt down, or test limits, they are often tired, hungry, thirsty, sick, or overstimulated. These "core conditions" account for a huge part of children's so-called naughtiness.

Lack of impulse control: Ever say, "Don't throw that!" and watch your kid throw it anyway? The researchers Tarullo, Obradovic, and Gunnar explain the behavior this way: "The brain regions involved in self-control are immature at birth and are not fully mature until the end of adolescence, which helps to explain why developing self-control is such a long, slow process" (2009, 31).

Developmental stages: There is a sizable gap between what many parents assume young children can do and what child development research shows about their abilities. For example, 71 percent of parents in one study believed that a child should be able to share and take turns by age 3, but this skill does not develop until children are between three and four years old. Fifty-six percent of parents in the study believed that children under the age of 3 have enough impulse control to resist the desire to do something forbidden, whereas most children do not master this skill until age 3½ or 4 (Zero to Three, 2016).

Response to inconsistent limits: Imagine you are blindfolded and have to feel your way around to determine the boundaries of a room. Now imagine the confusion you would feel if the walls of the room were not fixed but kept moving when you pushed on them. Kids need to learn the boundaries for their behavior, and they do it by "feeling around" with behaviors that test those boundaries. If you let kids jump off the couch sometimes but not always, they will keep jumping until they've figured out where you set the limit on that behavior.

Necessary developmental tasks: Seemingly "naughty" behaviors are often necessary steps toward kids' independence. For example, Erik Erikson's (1963) model posits that toddlers try to do things for themselves, and that preschoolers take initiative and carry out their own plans. Even though it's annoying when a child picks your tomatoes while they're still green, cuts their own hair, or makes a mess while slathering jelly when making their own sandwich, they're doing exactly what they are supposed to be doing — trying to carry out their own plans.

Strengths and weak spots: Children's strengths and passions or weak spots may cause them to have more pronounced behaviors, good or not so good. An oldest son, for example, may be very proud to help out with tasks that his siblings can't do yet. After helping his dad in the sandwich shop, the boy carefully carries the sandwich to the car. When the dad says, "Okay, give me the sandwich," the boy hesitates — not because he is naughty, but because while he's holding it he's in his element, being Dad's special helper. Another child may be highly competitive and motivated to be first, which drives her to work hard at school and sports. When she goes hiking with her family, at first she's stuck at the back, trying to catch up. She finally takes the lead and starts to run ahead. Her mom calls out "Stop!" but she keeps going because now she's first, which is important to her.

Understanding children's behavior does not excuse it. Gently setting consistent limits helps kids develop more positive behavior patterns. But maybe when we think about these factors, we can avoid thinking of kids as naughty and instead think of them as responding to circumstances, growing, and working through stuff, just as adults are. Maybe we can respond with a bit more compassion.

Snack Time

Brenda noticed that her son's behavior deteriorated right before lunch and dinner. When he started doing things wrong, she learned to ask herself, "Oh, man, does he need to eat?" and got him a snack. She also started feeding him at shorter intervals.

It's What We Signed Up For

Greta was at her chiropractor's office getting her back adjusted, with her two kids waiting beside the table, when she heard, "Mom! Mia bit me!" Greta was embarrassed and ready to jump up when the chiropractor said, "This is the gig, isn't it? This is all part of the gig — them doing this stuff, us teaching them a better way. It's what we signed up for." Greta nodded. The situation was still terrible, but her chiropractor's balanced view of kids' development made it feel like a terrible she could handle in that moment.

TRY THIS

Name one of your child's behaviors that you believe may be at least partially due to a developmental phase or to being tired, hungry, or overstimulated.

77 Make a Plan for Handling Arguments and Transitions

After a difficult situation has come up, like an argument between your kids, make a plan for how you'll handle it next time. Say the kids are playing nicely while you clean up breakfast. Eight seconds later, you hear one of them saying, "I want that! It's mine!" and the other one protesting, "No, mine!" Both want to put in the last puzzle piece or ride the rocking horse. If you have a plan, you may feel more prepared to defuse the situation calmly.

Here are some ways to deal with arguments:

Prepare: Before a playdate or free play with siblings, ask, "What toys are you excited to share with Olivia?" or "If you and Olivia want the same toy, what could you do?"

Remind kids of problem-solving phrases: "Can I have a turn when you're done?" "Can we set the timer so I can have a turn?"

Give kids attention when they're playing nicely: Look up not just when someone yells, "Ow!" or "Mine!" but also when they're co-operating.

Help kids reconnect: After a spat, have kids cool off, make amends, and talk about what they will do differently another time.

Appreciate the drama: While most of us hate conflicts, it's during dramas that kids get to practice working things out, standing up for themselves, coping with not getting their way, forgiving, and making up.

And here are suggestions for defusing arguments between parents and kids, such as how and when to leave a place where they're having fun.

Discuss the rules ahead of time: Before you arrive somewhere, ask your kids to describe the rules for when you're there. One rule may be, "When I say it's time to go, we all have to go right away, even if we don't want to." Then give an example: "What if you're doing something you really love doing, like going down the fire pole, and you don't want to go, and I say it's time to leave?" The kids will probably shout, "Go anyway!"

Figure out a fun way to leave: Ask kids to choose a code word for you to say when it's time to go. When they hear that word, they should run toward the nearest door. Suppose the code is "frog legs." Ask, "What are we going to do when we hear 'frog legs'?" "Run to the nearest door! We'll leave nicely and hop to our car, just like froggies!"

Leave fifteen minutes early: If you are all having a delightful time, preserve the positive memory by leaving while you're still having fun. Leaving fifteen minutes closer to nap and snack time can make the difference between a meltdown and a smooth transition.

Give an early warning: Some kids appreciate warnings, such as, "Five more minutes!" or "One last thing!" For other kids, however, this may cause anxiety; do what works for your kids.

Add a ritual: Have kids say, "Bye park!" or get a drink from the drinking fountain when they leave. Offer the same favorite snack, such as an apple or graham crackers, every time you leave. Let kids take a photo of a favorite swing, blow bubbles, name one thing they want to tell Grandma or Grandpa about, or choose something they want to do when they come back next time.

Give each kid a job for the way home: "Sally, you get to pick the music today. We can listen to rock and roll or Sesame Street songs. Clare, put your hand on the ceiling when everyone is buckled in. Jim, I want you to count the flags on the way home. Ann, could you pass out the water bottles to everyone? Carrie, choose if you want the car temperature to be hot or cold."

Ask children for ideas to make the situation easier for them: "I know we have such a great time at the library, but sometimes you get sad when it's time to leave. Do you have any ideas about how we could leave nicely?"

TRY THIS

Think of a difficult situation with your kids that could use some creative ideas for doing things differently.

Build a Joyful Relationship with Your Partner

78 Make Yourself Happy (instead of Relying on Your Partner to Do It)

A partner can't make you happy. It's up to you to do the things that keep you healthy and bright. Take care of yourself through healthy eating, exercise, sleeping, breaks, hobbies, meaningful work, and friendships. It's easy for parents to drift away from their support networks and later wish that their partners could fill the roles that best friends, moms, dads, or colleagues used to fill, and then feel disappointed when the partners don't do it as well.

A Need to Reconnect with Friends and Passions

Maddy and her husband moved from Seattle to Rhode Island when their kids were two and four. She worked long days and had wanted to spend all her free time with her kids while they were young. A few years later, Maddy felt increasingly unhappy that her husband wanted to spend weekends hanging around the house and watching sports, while she loved weekend road trips, hiking, and skiing. She realized that in the past, even after their marriage, she had done many of those things with her friends, not her husband. She had lost touch with most of her old friends and hadn't found many new close ones yet. It wasn't so much that her husband was doing something wrong as that she needed to make or rekindle friendships and do the things she loved.

TRY THIS

Identify the number-one thing you could do for yourself this week that would help you be more healthy and bright.

79 Keep Talking (and Share Emotional Dialogue)

Give your partner fifteen minutes of "complete presence" each day where you are looking at each other, really listening, and truly engaged. During this time, share "yes moments" — what you enjoyed about the day and what went well. Also use this time to build positive interactions, such as listening, appreciating, being affectionate, or showing interest, that will help you attain the "magic ratio" of relationship interactions (Gottman, cited in Poulsen, 2008). The "magic ratio" refers to research suggesting that as long as there are five times as many positive interactions between partners as there are negative, the relationship will be stable (Gottman, cited in Lisitsa, 2012).

Instead of replying to "How was your day?" with a terse "Fine" or "Good," challenge yourselves to share significant events and emotions. It can be hard to open these conversations if you're not in the habit. Consider trying one of these starter phrases:

"I'm sad [or scared, mad, or worried]. Could I talk this out with you?"

"I'm upset. I don't want you to try to fix it — I need to sort this out for myself. But would you mind listening for a minute?"

"This situation with my coworker is getting me down. Could I bounce some ideas off you?"

"I had a hard day. Would it be okay if I vent for a minute? ... Thanks for listening."

Avoid the alternative, simply dumping on your partner:

"You'll never believe what happened at work today. First, this! Then this! Can you believe that BS?"

"I'm so tired of cleaning when the kids just dump everything out again! I'm sick of this!"

Talk about things that you want to change in your relationship too. As Lisitsa (2012) writes on the *Gottman Relationship Blog*, "A relationship without conflict would not be able to move forward." While many people believe that they should bring up a relationship issue only if it's a really big deal, research suggests that the opposite is true: successful couples don't bottle things up. Instead they allow each other to complain and then work together to address the little issues between them (Fry, cited in Goudreau, 2015; Lisitsa, 2012).

TRY THIS

Think about whether you and your partner talk for at least fifteen minutes a day. Do you notice any patterns to your conversations?

80 Enjoy the Five Active Ingredients of Date Night

Many parents put the majority of their effort toward their kids and don't save much energy for each other. They are surprised when, following years of disconnection or ignoring, one person is enchanted by an extramarital affair or itching with restlessness or discontent. Make time for just the two of you amid the shuffle of Pinterest projects and pee-wee T-ball.

Many marriages end because of a loss of intimacy and connection, especially ten to twelve years into the marriage (Couples Training Institute, n.d.). Often, couples begin to silently drift apart much earlier, when one person starts to feel unhappy with the lack of closeness — less intimacy, conversation, time spent together, and expression of appreciation for one another. The biggest reason couples give for neglecting their relationships after having kids is that there's just not enough time. But it doesn't take a *lot* of time.

Regular date nights are one of the best ways to stay close. Stan Tatkin, the author of *Wired for Love*, argues that "the installation of happy memories" is crucial to a strong relationship. By "actively creating playful, happy, and bonding moments with each other," you "mutually amplify positive states" and create a pleasurable surge in dopamine, a feel-good neurochemical (Tatkin, 2011). Couples who devote time to one another at least once a week are more likely to have high-quality relationships and less likely to divorce (Wilcox and Dew, 2012). Couples who spend more time together also report higher levels of communication, sexual satisfaction, and commitment (Wilcox and Dew, 2012). A survey conducted by OnePoll.com found that going on three date nights per month was linked to being happily married (Daily Mail Reporter, 2014). However, many people do not make one-on-one time a priority.

In the rare moments when the kids are in bed early, sneak in mini dates. Make a list of things to do ahead of time so that when you do get a little unexpected free time, you can make it count. Make dinner together, taste wine, play a game, watch a movie, cook on the grill, or do other things you enjoy. Go out on dates with your partner at least twice a month.

The National Marriage Project (Wilcox and Dew, 2012) lists five "active ingredients" for date night:

Communication: Date nights limit distractions and allow couples to discuss the things that are important to them, foster intimacy, and "build a sense of communion" (Wilcox and Dew, 2012). While you might need to discuss a daughter's birthday party or who will repaint the bathroom, talking about more emotional topics on dates is essential. One way to do this is by building what the Gottman Institute calls love maps, exercises that allow couples to deepen their understanding of each other's inner worlds and move communication beyond "We need to fix the water heater" and "Should we get rid of cable?" The Gottman Love Maps App is one tool that can facilitate the process.

Novelty: Date nights let you enjoy fun, active, exciting, or unusual experiences that nurture shared interests and help you avoid taking each other for granted (Wilcox and Dew, 2012). Go new places, such as the batting cages, high school football games, country line dancing, hiking, or to plays. Choose activities that are "satisfying, stress-free, and increase closeness." Don't drag your partner along on the things *you* like to do. Relationship quality is best sustained when partners both want to share the activity (Girme, Overall, and Faingataa, 2014).

Eros, or romantic love: Date nights are one means of engaging in romantic activities together, rekindling spark, flirting or making playful romantic overtures, and fostering intimate and sexual connection (Social Issues Research Centre, 2004; Wilcox and Dew, 2012).

Commitment: Date nights show that you put each other first and remain dedicated to a sense of togetherness (Wilcox and Dew, 2012). True commitment means "doing what it takes to make the relationship thrive...even when it's not going well for you" or you are "not getting your way" in certain areas (Wolpert, 2012). Show commitment by planning, showing up on time, and being fully present. Spending special time with your partner acknowledges that your primary relationship will always remain important, even after additions to your family.

De-stressing: Taking time apart from family life can relieve symptoms of burnout and reenergize couples (Wilcox and Dew, 2012).

Engaging in lighthearted activities together releases stress, freeing you up to enjoy and support each other.

Go on a date — breakfast, lunch, dinner, coffee, or an adventure — at least a few times per month. Even if it's only for an hour, time alone together is fundamentally different from your time with kids. It helps you avoid becoming only coparenting or cohouseholding units.

Some ideas for dates:

Go bowling. Drink cheap beer or soda and eat junk food. Dress in your favorite bowling outfit with as many colors as possible and fix your hair in eighties styles.

Go for a hike. Make unique trail mixes for each other with ingredients you think your partner would like.

Play a board game. Talk trash. Be competitive.

Attend a high school football game, minor league baseball game, or fall football game together. Take selfies. Cheer loudly.

Go on a boat ride — a short canoe or kayak trip, a water taxi ride, a riverboat architecture tour, or a dinner cruise.

Build a snowman or go sledding. Warm up by a fire.

Go to a thrift store and choose one object (costing less than five dollars) that you think your partner would like. Be sneaky. Wrap it in newspaper and surprise them with it outside the store.

Go out for ice cream and ride bikes on a trail you've never explored.

Look at dream vacation destinations. Choose one you want to visit for your birthday twenty years from now.

Go fishing, even if you don't use any bait. Bring a comfy chair and a book to read while you're waiting for the fish to bite.

The One Thing They Didn't Cut Back On

David and Kathy treasured their date-night dinners. When David lost his job as a truck driver, they cut back on everything from cable to their kids' swimming lessons, but they still paid their babysitter so they could get their two hours of time alone together. "It's the highlight of my week," David noted. "And it will keep my spirits high as I'm looking for a new job."

TRY THIS

Plan a fun date with your partner in the next month or two.

81 Forgive

Forgive your partner for working late, spending money differently than you, or not parenting the exact same way you do. In the chaos of working late and cleaning gutters, you may get upset at a partner for little things and not have the time to resolve them. In addition to forgiving, use the complementary skill set of apologizing and repairing when *you* say or do things that are out of line or hurtful. Recalling the fact that you screw up too — that everyone does — may help you muster more empathy and forgive more easily.

Nursing a grudge can affect your heart rate, blood pressure, and overall health and stress levels (Witvliet, Ludwig, and Van der Laan, 2001; Worthington, 2004). Research suggests that when partners hurt each other, they experience a relationship shift that moves them from a spirit of cooperation and benevolence into one of competition, keeping score, and harping on the past. Forgiving one's partner is essential to restoring cooperation and producing a "net positive" feeling from which one can generate goodwill (Fincham, Hall, and Beach, 2006; Worthington, 2004).

Forgiveness can refer to shifts in internal emotions, in external behaviors, or both. For example, you may say "I forgive you," but still feel angry inside, or you may feel like you have let things go but don't want to admit it because you don't want it to happen again (Exline and Baumeister, 2000). To forgive, it may be helpful to fully honor and express your feelings, create a boundary to minimize the likelihood of your getting hurt again, and use a ritual to symbolically show that you are moving on (for example, by making a gesture to promote goodwill). Acknowledge that while at times a person may feel repentant (sorry about something they did), at other times they may not. There may be an impasse that just won't allow for mutual understanding, and you must move forward without the closure that agreement or an apology can sometimes bring.

Stitches

Marissa was at work while her husband took their three-year-old daughter to the park. Her daughter fell and needed stitches in her forehead. Marissa met her husband and daughter at the urgent care doctor's and cringed through the difficult procedure. For a few weeks after, Marissa made jabbing, accusatory comments to her husband that revealed her anger. She felt he had let the child fall, even though it had been an accident. She finally realized that holding this grudge wasn't fair and that she had to let it go, or it would start to corrode their relationship. She talked with her husband about her feelings, and he agreed to be more careful. The next day, she could acknowledge, for the first time in weeks, some of the ways he was taking great care of their daughter. She thanked him for reading her books, making her breakfast, and playing trains with her.

Similar to forgiving, but not quite the same, is accepting the fact that there will be a number of problems in your relationship that may not be worked out. The researcher John Gottman reports that

69 percent of relationship problems are "perpetual" problems based on personality differences between partners (Gottman, 2015). Letting things go, agreeing to disagree, and focusing on positives are important tools for coping with problems that may never go away.

Countertops

Dennis made dinner every night, and his partner, Leah, washed the dishes. Without fail, every pot, pan, and dish was clean by the next morning. However, Leah never cleaned the countertops — it wasn't even on her radar to do so. When Dennis saw crumbs, dried ketchup, or random potato peels on the counter the next morning, he felt frustrated that she had not cleaned them up, too, since he saw it as part of the kitchen cleanup task. When he realized that his daily frustration about the dirty countertops was preventing him from appreciating everything Leah did do to help, he finally let it go.

TRY THIS

Think of something your partner has done or not done that has made you upset. Have you expressed all your feelings about what happened? How would your behavior look different if you made a choice to forgive your partner or simply to let go of a pattern of frustration?

82　Be Thoughtful and Playful

We become what we repeatedly do. — SEAN COVEY

When participants in one relationship study were asked, "What two things do you like best about your relationship?" they mentioned small words, gestures, and actions — like having their partner bring them a cup of tea in bed or cooking a meal for them. Though conventional gifts like flowers and chocolates were appreciated, respondents emphasized the thoughtfulness of the way the gift was presented and its meaning more than the gift itself (Gabb et al., 2013).

Here are a few ways to be generous, kind, thoughtful, and playful:

Greetings and goodbyes: Start and end each day with a positive, sweet, or gracious remark such as "Hi, beautiful, thanks for getting up last night with the baby. I know it's hard to have such disrupted sleep, and you are so patient."

Touch: Parents often can't get enough of holding children on laps, rocking, or cuddling. It can be harder to keep up physical contact with a partner. Touches throughout the day refresh your connection.

Compliments: Compliment your partner with "I love your enthusiasm for life," "You are such a hard worker," or "You're a great listener." Research suggests that complimenting a person's intrinsic qualities means more to them than complimenting their deeds and accomplishments (Gordon, 2010).

Humor and playfulness: Playfulness, a sense of humor, and being fun-loving are extremely attractive traits to both men and women, ranking above other traits such as "good earning capacity" and "attractive" (Chick, Yarnal, and Purrington, 2012). Joke around, take bets on who can get the baby to burp first, or take before-and-after photos of your house on the day of a boisterous kids' party.

Holiday rituals: On busy holidays, don't forget little gestures for your partner, such as a well-written card, a holiday stocking, or breakfast in bed. Give a small surprise gift: research suggests that most people prefer gifts that are unexpected and appreciate the gift giver more when gifts are unexpected (Venkatraman and Berman, 2015). Create traditions for celebrating each other's birthdays. Create couple rituals, such as having hot chocolate together on Christmas Eve after the kids go to bed, hearing live music on the Fourth of July, or running a 5K on New Year's Day.

Love letters: Write love letters. Describe in detail at least three things you love about your partner. Include a romantic detail or phrase that only the two of you know. Recall a favorite memory and name something you're looking forward to doing together: this week, this year, or when you grow old. Add a unique or mushy closing like "From the one who's adored you from the first time I saw you at the beach."

Hello from The Business Hotel in Oklahoma

Tom traveled a lot for work. He kept postcard stamps in his wallet and sent his wife a sweet postcard from every city he visited, even if he knew it would arrive after he was already home.

TRY THIS

Think of a kind or thoughtful thing you could do for your partner this week.

83 Use Thank-Yous to Boost Your Relationship

Research suggests that gratitude is a powerful booster for romantic relationships (Algoe, Gable, and Maisel, 2010). Gratitude predicts how happy someone will be in their marriage, improves levels of commitment to a marriage (Barton, Futris, and Nielsen, 2015), improves the quality of intimate relationships (Parnell, 2015), and makes it more likely that partners will stay together over time (Gordon et al., 2012). Gratitude also counteracts and protects against the negative effects of arguing (Barton, Futris, and Nielsen, 2015) and generates reciprocal goodwill (Gordon et al., 2012).

Don't just feel grateful for a partner: say thank you regularly. Thank your partner for working, changing diapers, being a good listener, or doing chores. Say thank you through messages, by email, on sticky notes around your house, on voicemail, with a homemade or store-bought card, with flowers, or with a special meal. Record ongoing thank-yous in a bedside journal that you and your partner can read and contribute to or use the Gottman Institute's Give Appreciation app.

Although gratitude can work wonders, it may be hard to keep it flowing. The psychologist Thomas Gilovich argues that two "enemies" of gratitude are *negativity bias* — "our tendency to see things that are holding us back more clearly than the good things that are pushing us forward" — and *adaptation* — "We tend to get used to things, which often renders the good things invisible" (cited in J. Smith, 2014).

You've Won!

Nick puts the laundry through the washer and dryer, and his wife Rosa sorts it and puts it away. One day, Rosa taped a note on the washing machine with tickets to a soccer match that she knew he would love. She wrote, "For doing the 1,000th load of laundry, you've won two tickets to the Gold Cup!"

TRY THIS

Think of one thing you want to thank your partner for and a creative way you could do it.

84 Send Positive Text Messages

One study has shown that texting between partners can either help or hurt a relationship. For women, using texts to apologize, work out differences, or make decisions was associated with lower relationship quality. For men, too-frequent texting was also associated with lower relationship quality. On the positive side, researchers found that using text messages to express affection actually enhances relationships and creates a stronger partner attachment. Sending a loving text was even more strongly related to relationship satisfaction than receiving one (Schade et al., 2013). Use text messages to build closeness:

Send a *compliment,* such as "I love your enthusiasm for life!" or "Thanks for getting the kids to school on time this morning."

Send a *thank-you,* such as "Thanks for doing all that laundry last night. I know you were tired," or "Thanks for shoveling our snow as well as our neighbors' sidewalk."

Share a *fond memory* such as, "I had so much fun with you at the New Year's 5K — let's do that again!" or "Wasn't it fun to go to Chinatown? I was just thinking about how much fun we had trying new foods together."

Share a *bit of joy,* such as "I had the best time hiking in the woods with the kids. We even saw a deer, and their faces just lit up when it crossed our path." Or "The new customer signed on at work — so excited!"

TRY THIS

Talk to your partner about positive texting, and send at least three positive text messages tomorrow.

85 Go to Bed When Your Partner Does

*For many couples, that time in bed before going to sleep
is sometimes the most precious time and the most important time.*
— WENDY TROXEL

A full 75 percent of couples do not go to bed at the same time, usually because one person is surfing the web, working, or watching TV. Partners tend to stop going to bed at the same time about three and a half years into a relationship (Cliff, 2015).

Going to bed at the same time, with plenty of time to connect before falling asleep, can offer significant benefits. Larson, Crane, and Smith (1991) found that "couples whose wake and sleep patterns were mismatched (e.g., an evening person married to a morning person) reported significantly less marital adjustment, more marital conflict, less time spent in serious conversation, less time spent in shared activities and less frequent sexual intercourse than matched couples."

Another reason to go to bed at the same time is that, according to one study, it makes female partners view daytime interactions more positively the next day. That's a pretty amazing effect for such a simple, easy gesture of togetherness. The study found that simply getting a good night's sleep had the same effect for male partners (Hasler and Troxel, 2010).

Bedtime is often time for cuddling, which helps people feel nurtured and relaxed. It can also inspire feelings of love, happiness, comfort, satisfaction, bonding, and feeling appreciated (Van Anders et al., 2013). When couples talk after sex — "pillow talk" — the release of the "love hormone" or "cuddle hormone" oxytocin can make it more likely that they will disclose positive feelings for each other, a behavior that is associated with trust, relationship satisfaction, and closeness (Denes, 2012).

Keep your cell phone out of the bedroom. Looking at your phone while talking to your partner can lower relationship satisfaction (Roberts and David, 2016). When drifting off to sleep, consider staying close. Although many happy couples do not even share a bed, one study found that partners who slept less than an inch apart were more likely to be content with their relationship than those maintaining a gap wider than thirty inches. Couples who made physical contact through the night were also happier than those with a no-touching rule while sleeping (Perry, 2014).

TRY THIS

If you don't usually go to bed at the same time as your partner, discuss the far-reaching, long-term benefits of doing so, at least sometimes, and see if they're up for it.

86 Communicate While Calm, Clear-Headed, and Rested

In a perfect world, no one would ever need to put off a difficult conversation with a significant other. We would be Zen-like all the time, speaking from our hearts, steering clear of accusations, and crystal clear on what we wanted to have happen next. We would be stellar listeners and paraphrasers and eager to make things right with the people we love the most. Since instead we are human, tabling a topic about which we are angry or "putting it off until our higher self can take the lead," can be an effective tool for communicating.

When angry, we experience a primal urge toward fighting, flight, or fawning. In *flight* mode, we storm out, sulk, withdraw, avoid, ignore, or even separate. In *fight* mode, we shout, accuse, shame, guilt, blame, belittle, bring up issues from the past, or say hurtful things we don't mean. When we *fawn*, we appease the other person without getting our own needs met.

A study by John Gottman reports that the more "'diffusely

physiologically aroused' (in fight, flight, or fawn mode) someone is during a conflict conversation, the more his or her marital satisfaction is likely to decline during a period of three years." Taking a twenty-minute break during which couples stopped talking and read magazines "dramatically changed the discussion so that people had access to their sense of humor and affection" (Gottman, 2015). Even if you don't have a temper, you will benefit from a few deep breaths to bring mindfulness to your feelings before you express them. "I want to talk about this respectfully with you, but I can't right now. Can we talk in twenty minutes [or in an hour, or in the morning]?"

Communication may also be hindered by a lack of sleep. Your ability to manage your emotions is greatly diminished when you are short of sleep (Goldstein and Walker, 2014). In one study, people who were sleep-deprived showed greater subjective stress, anxiety, and anger following exposure to a low stressor than a control group that was well-rested (Minkel et al., 2012). Lack of sleep has also been shown to decrease the expression of positive emotion and increase the expression of negative emotion (McGlinchey et al., 2011). Couples fight more and have a harder time resolving conflict if even one partner slept poorly the night before. When you get annoyed, Amie Gordon suggests reminding yourself that "it's not him/her, it's the lack of sleep" (Gordon, 2016).

TRY THIS

Identify your typical response to conflict: fight, flight, fawn, or calm and clear-headed?

87 Respond to Your Partner's Efforts toward Closeness

Be attentive to your partner's efforts to engage with you. According to John Gottman, partners make "requests for connection" (also called "bids") throughout the day. They might be as subtle as saying, "I met Steve for lunch today." It's not that the partner particularly wants to talk about Steve or the lunch: rather, he or she wants the partner to show interest or support that will lead to connection. The partner has a choice: to ignore the bid or "turn away" (for example, by saying, "Uh-huh," while texting) or to answer the bid or "turn toward" (responding with "How did it go? Tell me about it!") (Gottman, cited in E. Smith, 2014). Sometimes a bid is more overt, such as, "I was thinking we should go on a date." The partner may turn away — "How's that gonna go? We don't even have a babysitter!" — or turn toward — "Yes, I'd love to. Let's make that happen. I'll ask my mom to babysit." Gottman found that couples who stayed together after six years turned toward bids 86 percent of the time, whereas couples who divorced after six years had turned toward bids only 33 percent of the time (Gottman, 2015).

Have you ever read the children's book called *More Spaghetti, I Say?* One little guy wants to play with his friend, but she's too busy scarfing spaghetti to play with him. When she finally wants to play with him, he's too busy eating spaghetti to play with *her*. This happens all the time in relationships. Every couple endures periods when they grow apart. They stop making an effort to go on dates, write birthday cards, or even hug. One person makes an effort to reconnect, but it doesn't work because the other person is feeling down, holding a grudge, or just distracted. A little while later, the other person makes an effort, but by then, his or her partner is no longer thinking about it or is too hurt by the previous lack of response to engage. It's like having one tire grip the snow while the other spins without traction: the car doesn't move. Time goes by without any real progress, even though both people feel they really tried. The problem is, they did not try at the same time, and each failed to respond to the other's efforts.

When one person puts effort into a relationship, it's essential for the other to acknowledge that effort and reciprocate as fast as possible.

TRY THIS

List the most common distractions in your relationship that keep you and your partner from acknowledging each other's efforts.

88 Notice What Your Partner Is Teaching You

Our partners can be our best teachers. We often choose partners that have traits and skills that balance or complement our own. At times, the teaching is overt, like how to rock climb or put together a dresser. Other times, they inspire us to be better just by example. A partner may model patience in situations that make us crazy. She may be good with people when we feel antisocial. He might be attuned to his health in a way we would like to be.

Drop Everything and Show Up

Julie's husband, Peter, had flown to North Dakota to see his cousin, who had just been diagnosed with cancer. He flew to Arizona to visit his grandmother when she'd had a terrible fall. He had driven downtown on a Friday afternoon to be with a friend who'd just broken up with his girlfriend. So when Julie's best friend six states away had a stillbirth, she booked the next ticket out to visit her and stayed for three days.

Before she had known Peter, she hadn't known how important it was to show up — how much it meant to somebody if you could be there during hard times.

TRY THIS

Name one thing your partner has taught or is teaching you about life.

89 Support the Relationship between Your Partner and Your Kids

Help your children see their other parent in the best possible light — the light of your love. Thank your partner in front of your kids, and encourage them to do the same:

> "Let's say thanks to your mom for fixing your bike. Isn't she handy? She can fix so many things!"
> "Thanks for working all day to make money to buy this yummy food, Mom!"
> "See how fast Dad cleaned? Thanks, Dad, now we have room to run around!"

Point out to your kids your partner's positive traits:

> "Doesn't Dad do the funniest voices when he's reading you books? Isn't he fun to read books with?"
> "I see how Mom brushes your hair very gently and holds

it so it doesn't hurt. Now your hair looks so shiny and smooth."

"Look how Dad packed the whole car while we were sleeping so we could leave right away for vacation. Wow, he was really working hard!"

Help your kids make cards and art projects for your partner:

"Dad is really going to love this card we're making for him with Rice Chex and glue!"

Tell your children funny, endearing stories about your partner's past:

"This one time when I was sick, Mom took really good care of me. She even made me a get-well basket with homemade chicken soup."

"Your dad used to be a catcher in baseball games, just like that guy in that picture. He was so good at throwing that he could whip that ball across the whole field!"

Make room for your partner to take each child out for some special one-on-one time:

"Why don't you take John out to the baseball game, just the two of you? I can stay home with the other two."

"If you want to just take Jane to the beach today, I will take John shopping with me."

Let your kids help you surprise your partner:

"Hey, I've got a great idea! Let's make Mom breakfast in
bed. She'll love that!"
"Why don't we wash Daddy's car while he's at work?
He'll be so surprised!"

Sing your partner's praises to grandparents, friends, coworkers, or neighbors as well. If you are coparenting with a person who
is not your current partner, it is still important to note positives (or
at least abstain from negatives) about that person.

TRY THIS

Think of one thing you could do to strengthen your
kids' relationship with their other parent.

90 Surprise Your Partner

Indifference and neglect often do much more damage
than outright dislike. — J. K. ROWLING

Surprises add spark to your relationship and communicate how much you care. You may think, "I treat my partner well on a daily basis, so why do I need to surprise him or her?" With an unexpected treat or gesture, you articulate that your relationship is worth making a special effort for. It deserves even more nourishment than everyday life — even a kind and loving life — allows. The "newness" enlivens what's between you.

Sometimes people are consumed with thinking about what they are not getting, so it's hard for them to think about something extra they could give. People also feel that they do not have time to plan one more thing. But they often underestimate the immense power that a simple surprise holds. Surprises can lead to greater intimacy, tender interactions, and contentment. They can act as a catalyst to make a whole host of other relationship patterns shift for the better.

If your partner is truly surprised and warmed by something nice you do, you'll notice physical signs — raised eyebrows, wide eyes, dropped jaw, or large grin — associated with a hit of positive neurochemical reactions. You'll get a good feeling too, from being the giver.

Here are some ideas for surprising your partner:

Send a message through an unusual means, such as on Facebook Messenger, through mail sent to a hotel they will be staying at, in the mail to your house disguised as a bill, or written in the bathroom with washable crayons.

Do a chore that is typically your partner's job, like taking out the garbage.

Draw a morning bubble bath for your partner and serve a cup of coffee with it.

Put a note in your partner's wallet, car, or briefcase.

Get up early with your kids and sneak out of the house to the park so your partner can sleep in.

Book a babysitter and surprise your partner with a restaurant meal, a trip to the batting cages, or a baseball game.

Record a super-sweet voice message for your partner.

Bring home your partner's favorite ice cream or takeout food.

Get your partner's car washed or detailed.

When you're away for work or with friends, bring your partner a funny souvenir trinket.

Think of something you used to do when you first met. If you loved going out for a Mexican breakfast, take your partner out for huevos rancheros. If you used to go to poetry slams, find one to attend.

Arrange to do something that your partner loves doing but you typically don't or won't do (like picking berries or watching an animated film).

Show up at your partner's workplace to take them to lunch.

If your partner springs a surprise outing on you, don't argue — go gratefully. Acknowledge it, share what it meant for you, or say thank you aloud or with a handmade card. Draw a stick figure picture of yourself enjoying the surprise. Give a surprise back. Step up and try to be just as creative, giving, and thoughtful as the other person was (if not more).

TRY THIS

Think about when you last surprised your partner. Which idea from the above list would your partner enjoy the most?

91 Ask Novel Questions

Thoughtful, funny, or meaningful questions brighten conversations and help you grow as a couple. They help you and your partner get to know each other better, dream together, and shape your joint future. Although you could simply ask questions, it may also be fun to play a version of the Newlywed Game, in which you write down your answers to a question, write down what you think your partner would say, and then compare them, giving each other points for matching answers.

> If you had to write a book or a magazine article, what would it be about?
>
> Who is the most "out there in a good way" person you've ever met?
>
> What social cause is most important to you?
>
> What's your favorite spot in our city?

If you could see one major sporting event this year, what
would it be?

If you could start over and have a different career, what
would you do?

Which three people (besides me) do you think know you
the best?

Who was your best friend as a child, and why?

What's your idea of a perfect date?

Who is one of the best listeners you know?

Where do you want to live when we retire?

What three traits would you most want your kids to have?

Who is a person who brought out the worst in you at one
time?

What's the most scared you've ever been?

What's something you want to make absolutely sure you
do in the next five years?

What's been a moment of complete grace or awe in your
life?

What's the most exceptional spiritual experience you've
ever had?

Who are two friends you expect to have forever, who are
most likely to be there at the end?

What was your favorite vacation?

Which car fits your personality the best?

If you had to leave this town tomorrow, what would you
regret not doing more of?

If you had to get a tattoo, what would you get?

What lesson do you seem to keep learning over and over?

What nicknames have you had?

If you have been lucky enough to find a great love, why not get to know that person even better?

TRY THIS

Think about how you and your partner could incorporate more novel questions into your time together.

92 Use Couples Counseling as a Romantic Retreat

Couples counseling is the ultimate indulgence. You might not have thought about it on a par with a three-layer chocolate cake or a bouquet of roses. You might think of it as the last resort before divorce, something you're forced to do because your partner wants you to change, a possible solution to your screaming matches, or what you might have to do if one of you had an affair. But couples counseling is not always about damage control: it's something the most enlightened, forward-thinking, fully conscious partners do by choice. It's a romantic, intentional approach to tending to one of your closest relationships, especially during times of great change.

Whereas the effects of most indulgences wear off quickly, couples counseling helps develop positive, long-lasting, life-affirming patterns. It helps you identify the best possible ways to support each other through tough times, communicate, and strengthen your bond. It can also help you open up and discuss issues on a deeper level. If you work on shifting communication patterns or other habits, you may become frustrated when you have changed, but your family system — the long-standing pattern of interactions you've established with your partner — hasn't. The family system may (in an effort to maintain homeostasis), sabotage any changes you try to make and pull you right back to the way you were before. Many couples who experience tensions wait until their children are older and things have settled down to seek help. But if you wait, patterns can become ingrained, and you may endure years of difficulty that could have been a lot happier. And if you decide that your relationship is truly over, counseling can also help you through a separation or divorce.

Here are a few ways to make the most of couples counseling:

Ask the miracle question: The miracle question is designed to help unstick ingrained negative patterns and complaints and identify exactly how you want things to be (De Jong and Berg, 2012). If a miracle occurred overnight in your relationship, and you woke up and found that everything that was a problem was magically fixed, what would your day look like? What would your partner be doing? What would you be doing? What would your exchanges entail?

The miracle question, which asks you to make believe that your life is already better, moves you from accusatory, backward-looking, blaming, or hopeless thinking into positive, goal-oriented thinking. It moves you from "He did this bad thing" and "I can't stand that about him" to identifying interactions that would make you feel content or loved (De Jong and Berg, 2012). "She would be listening to me when I talked about work instead of interrupting," "He would be planning dates for us," or "She would be initiating intimacy."

Remember why you fell in love: Think about your first few meetings or dates. What stood out? What drew you together or made you such a good match? What were some of your best times together? When things are good, what is it that's good?

Take stock of how each of you is doing individually: Are you happy? How is your health? What are you excited about? Are there any changes you want to make? What's been stressful or successful at work lately? Are you feeling connected to your friends and family? Sometimes people believe that an issue stems from their relationship when it really originates in themselves.

Think about a few things you could or should be doing differently: "I would bring up issues instead of brushing them under the rug," or "I would not complain about spending time with her family." If you acknowledge these issues, counseling sessions are less likely to get bogged down by complaints.

Small Changes

For years, Ray had worked insanely long hours for a large nonprofit that helped the homeless. He managed a large team of people and had immense passion and commitment. After having a child, his workaholism no longer fit with his family life. His wife, Wendy, became unhappy with his being gone for so many hours and distracted by his job even when he was home. In counseling, Ray started to see the detrimental effects of his constant work. He started making small changes — surprising Wendy and their baby with lunches together, listening to Wendy's feelings without getting defensive, and getting home for dinner every night.

TRY THIS

Think about whether couples counseling could be an indulgence or intentional retreat to strengthen your relationship during a tough time. Is there anything holding you back from pursuing it?

Build Joyful Relationships with Grandparents

93 Decide Together How Grandparents Will Be Involved

Grandparents can bring an abundance of joy to family life. Kids who form close relationships with adults other than their parents are likely to have higher self-esteem and to be more successful at school and work (Search Institute, 2005). Grandparents can be some of the most important adults in a child's life. A key predictor of the grandparent-grandchild relationship (besides living close to each other) is the quality of the relationships between the parents and grandparents (Dunifon and Bajracharya, 2012). If your relationship with your own parent(s) is strained, parenthood may be a time to help both sides air feelings and work toward healing.

Some grandparents want to be tremendously involved with childcare, outings, and visits. Others enjoy seeing grandkids only on special occasions. While some parents value and appreciate grandparents' help (and would sometimes like more), others would like more space and clearer boundaries. When the goals of parents and grandparents don't align, at least one party often feels frustrated or hurt by the mismatch. Communicate with grandparents about how time is spent, and appreciate the ways they do participate in your family's lives, even if they're not exactly what you wanted.

A few ideas for involving grandparents in children's activities:

Sign up for an activity or class that your kids can do with a grandparent, such as a fishing class at the arboretum, library story time, making a birdhouse at a Home Depot class, baking cupcakes in a park-district class, or taking a music class at the arts center.

Invite grandparents to your kids' sports game, school play, or music concert.

Go away for a weekend with grandparents.

Get a zoo or museum membership that lets grandparents take kids there.

Arrange for a sleepover for your kids at a grandparent's house.

Mention details about grandparents to your kids: "Did you know that Grandpa used to make sirens in a fire-truck factory?" or "Grandma sure loves to collect shells on the beach!" or "Did you know Grandpa built his house from scratch when he was younger?" or "Did you know Grandma lived in Poland before she came to live here?"

Help kids make thank-you cards when grandparents bake them banana bread or buy them a jacket.

Leave space for grandparents to develop their own relationships with your children. Don't hover.

Allow grandparents to indulge your kids (e.g., by giving them cookies for breakfast).

Make homemade presents for grandparents.

Install car seats or booster seats in grandparents' cars so they can take your kids somewhere if they want to.

Call grandparents on the phone and let children have individual conversations with them.

Plan some fun activities (such as art projects, playing with Play-Doh, or board games) for grandparents to do with your kids when they come over.

Teach your kids to be polite to their grandparents by giving them hugs, getting them a glass of water, or serving them dinner first.

Have grandparents pick up kids from school once in a while.

Invite grandparents to share an activity they love with your kids (like gardening or fishing).

Attend a parade with grandparents.

Ask grandparents to do a creative job, such as putting together a library for the baby's nursery.

Heart-to-Heart

Because of his girlfriend's drug addiction, Luke assumed full custody of his daughter, Anya, when she was just two months old. For the first few months, Luke's mother, Carol, had lived close to his Nevada home and helped him out in various ways, such as babysitting when he needed to work overtime or take a different shift. However, when Anya was six months old, Carol moved to California. When she came back for holidays, a part of Luke did not want to see her because he felt so angry and hurt that she had left him when he needed her the most. Luke had a heart-to-heart talk with his mother and told her how he was feeling. They worked out a schedule where she visited one weekend a month instead of just at the holidays.

TRY THIS

Recall some of the beautiful moments grandparents have spent with your kids. What's one other way you could involve them?

94 Honor the Unique Traits of Grandparents

Acknowledge that even if grandparents do things differently from you, they often interact with children in unique and enriching ways.

Here are some ways grandparents can make unique contributions to your family life:

Grandparents can invite *help*. "Pick these weeds over here," one grandpa says. "Good, now dig a hole here for the seeds." "Can you spray that lilac tree with the hose? Good, that's the way."

Grandparents can be *wise*. A grandma brought a small present for her granddaughter when it was her brother's birthday. After the girl watched her brother open about six gifts, she lit up when she realized that her grandma had brought her a little gift too.

Grandparents can be *patient*. A grandpa reads to his grandchildren slowly. He examines the pictures and asks the kids questions.

He colors slowly, walks slowly, and cooks carefully from scratch. When the kids are at their grandpa's, they seem more patient, too.

Grandparents can be *indulgent*. One grandma shows up with new pajamas, old Happy Meal toys, forty-year-old toys from her basement, ancient books from libraries that are closing, and new flip-flops. She sneaks the kids jelly beans and grape juice because she can.

Grandparents *can make the mundane exciting*. If you asked one grandpa's kids if they would rather go to the beach or do laundry with Grandpa, they'd probably pick the laundry. They love pretending the laundry basket is a delivery truck and delivering laundry to all the bedrooms.

Grandparents can be *humble*. One grandpa plays the student, the underdog, or the one who doesn't know how to do something. "Now where is the park from here?" he will say. "Oh, it's this way? Okay, you lead the way." "Now, how do you play this kind of game? Good, you show me."

Grandparents can be *creative*. One grandma gets out her button collection and engages the kids in sorting, feeling the smoothness of, and lining up buttons. She grabs the bag of rocks she collected at the beach and helps children make cards by gluing smooth stones onto paper. Then she dredges up a cardboard box from the recycling bin and carves it into a sailboat, which enlivens the afternoon.

Honor grandparents and others who have passed by emulating their positive qualities and keeping their traditions alive.

Angelo loves taking his own children to the bakery once in a while to let them choose a cookie, just like his grandma did for him.

Nina's grandmother was great at keeping kids busy and engaged doing jobs while she sorted laundry or did other chores. Her granddaughter remembers her while she tries to get her own chores done while giving her children jobs to help out.

Frank's grandmother's love for him transcended rules. She sneaked into the hospital to see him when he was sick and no visitors were allowed. Frank remembers her whenever he feels that fierce instinct to protect his own children.

Leslie loves to tell her kids stories about their grandfather, who passed. She brings up tidbits — that he hated peaches, flew in a tiny airplane with his pilot friend, loved animals, and drove a forklift. He was jolly and loving. Whenever her kids exude the same kind of jovial good nature, she thinks of him and sees that his spirit has been passed on. On his birthday, Leslie encourages her kids to do artwork that honors him, like painting a cake or a blue convertible (his favorite car).

Celeste's grandma taught her to knit. She loves dressing her kids in the little sweaters and hats she made with her grandma when she was young. Seeing them in the colorful knits makes her feel like her grandma is still around.

TRY THIS

Identify one legacy, something a grandparent does well or was known for, that you would like to remember or carry on.

Build Joyful Relationships with Friends

95 Accept Friendship Changes and Losses and Initiate New Friendships

When you have children, friendships are challenged and stretched in new ways. While some friendships may deepen, others may change or fade. Priorities, lifestyles, locations, and other factors shift so dramatically in parenthood that you may no longer click well with certain friends. Different parenting styles, challenging child behaviors, and children's schedules can make it tough to see friends. While changes in friendships are a natural and major consequence of any big life transition, they can be very painful. Forgive your friends or have open conversations when they become flaky, exhausted, or missing in action, and acknowledge that sometimes you may exhibit those very same traits. If nothing changes, honor your feelings of loss and try to move on.

Although you will likely lose some friends, parenthood provides a chance to strengthen existing friendships, revive old friendships, and develop new ones. Consider joining a playgroup, which can provide valuable social support for parents as well as kids. In one study, mothers who did not participate in an ongoing play-group were twice as likely to have no social support when their kids reached eight and nine years old, compared with mothers who "persistently participated" (Hancock et al., 2015). Find playgroups through Meetup groups, hospitals, religious institutions, or neighborhood newcomers' clubs.

Reaching Out

Raquel moved from Washington, DC, to North Carolina to be closer to her parents when her son was born, and she had to leave all her friends. Her maternity leave was the loneliest time of her life. She signed up for a new-mom yoga class and talked to everyone in it. She also began attending a hospital-based new-moms' support group and met a few more new people. It took about a year, but she eventually made a few new, solid friends who often got together on Sunday afternoons.

TRY THIS

Think about whether you lost or grew apart from a friend on becoming a parent. What do you think happened?

96 Invest Time in Friendships

It is one of the blessings of old friends that you can afford to be stupid with them. — Ralph Waldo Emerson

Friendships help you get through challenges and buffer you from stress. They help you explore, grow, and achieve more, broaden and build resources, and foster a sense of meaning (Feeney and Collins, 2015). Friendships satisfy important needs, including bonding and having someone to call on for comfort and to engage in activities that produce positive memories. Along with job satisfaction, satisfaction with one's friendships (not just the number of one's friends) has been identified as one of the two strongest predictors of life satisfaction (Gillespie et al., 2015).

Friendship is also an essential element in preserving mental health. Whether providing total acceptance, laughter, or an optimistic spin on things, friends help you maintain a positive state of mind. A meta-analysis of 148 studies also found that people with stronger social relationships were significantly more likely to live longer. This finding remained consistent across age, sex, health status, cause of death, and follow-up period (Holt-Lunstad, Smith, and Layton, 2010).

Investing time in friendships is a key predictor of their duration (Ledbetter, Griffin, and Sparks, 2007). However, the friendship researcher William Rawlins found that many middle-aged people reported that "they rarely had time to spend with their most valued friends, whether because of circumstances or through the age-old problem of good intentions and bad follow-through" (cited in Beck, 2015). To remedy this problem, arrange a standing dinner date with a friend at least once a month. Host a holiday party where everyone brings cans of food to donate to a shelter. Plan a canoe trip, a mud run, or a fall bike ride with old friends. Visit an out-of-town friend for a weekend.

And when your friends call you with invitations like this, call them back. Using data from 2 million people and 8 million phone calls, the physicists Cesar Hidalgo and Carlos Rodriguez-Sickert analyzed the structure of networks of friends and found that "the leading cause of persistent relationships is reciprocity — returning a friend's call" (Zyga, 2008).

Reflect on how well you reciprocate invitations from friends. If a friend says, "We should get together sometime," do you answer, "Great, how about Saturday?" If a friend invites you and your kid over for a playdate, do you invite her back two weeks later? If a friend gives you all her kid's old clothes for your daughter, do you find a way to repay her generosity? Also, take inventory of what you get back from friends. If you are sad or angry about a friend's lack of reciprocation, address it directly. "I'm feeling down about how little you ask me to get together. Mind if we talk about this?"

Or set a boundary like "I will ask this new friend to come over three times, then I need him to put in some effort too, or I need to move on." If your efforts at trying to make or keep a friend consistently fall flat, it can seriously sap your energy. Let it go, give yourself some space to grieve, and move forward with other relationships. Remember that it's not necessarily personal: research suggests that because of modern values and demands on people's time, dropping the ball in middle-aged friendships is common (Beck, 2015).

TRY THIS

Think of one outing you'd like to plan with a good friend this year.

97 Initiate Gestures of Friendship

The find-remind-bind theory of gratitude asserts that a simple thank-you can help you to find, deepen, and cement friendships (Algoe, 2012). Gestures of friendship, such as cards, small gifts, or homemade meals can do the same.

Charlotte sent her friend Wonder Woman socks to wear for her physical therapy sessions after knee surgery.

After a friend's mom had passed, Meara brought her meals for four weeks after the funeral.

When Ignacio's friend started a mail-order beef jerky company, Ignacio raved to his friends about it and reposted his friend's advertisements on his Facebook page.

Talya brought over warm chocolate chip cookies when her friend's baby was in the hospital.

Simon's friend started a daddy blog, and Simon made it
a point to make an encouraging comment on every
blog post.

Casimir mowed his friend's lawn after his friend was in-
jured in a car accident and needed a few weeks of recovery time.

Notice brief windows of opportunity in which you can offer
support. If a friend is sick, deliver soup or flowers. If he's feeling
blue, bring over some tea or a funny DVD. If she is dreading a long
road trip, drop off a pack of gum and your favorite music CD. If a
friend's dog died, send a card. Send a simple message: "I'm thinking of you," or "Just checking in about [that hard thing] — how
are you doing?" The power of thoughtfulness is increased tenfold
when a gesture is made at the exact moment when someone is feeling vulnerable or down.

TRY THIS

Think of a friend or acquaintance who's having a hard
time. What's a simple, kind gesture you could make to
help them?

98 Accept Every Invitation — or Add a "But"

If a friend invites you to an adults-only cocktail party, be there. If you've agreed to grab dinner with a friend at the end of a long day, show up. If someone asks you over for a Sunday afternoon playdate, make it happen.

If you need to say no, don't drop the invitation like a vase on the floor with a flat "Can't make it." Don't go on about the fabulous thing you're doing instead: "No can do, I'm going to an incredible concert that night!" For the sake of kindness, when you decline an invitation, always include a "but" as a counteroffer. It shows that even if you need to say no, you care deeply about the other person and value the relationship.

> "I can't meet you for dinner Saturday, but how about next Friday?"
>
> "We can't stay for dinner, but we'd love to come for lunch."

"I can't play tennis right now, but I'd love to play Wednesday."

"I can't call you back tonight, but I'll call you first thing tomorrow morning!"

"We can't visit for a week this year, but we would love to come for a long weekend."

"I can't come to your birthday happy hour, but I'd love to take you out another night."

TRY THIS

When your friends invite you to do something, ask yourself if you usually say yes. If you say no, do you suggest an alternative?

99 Recognize That What Helped You May Not Help Everyone

When you find your cure-all, your magic potion, or your "it" thing, it's tough to hold back from talking about it. You may rave about how your sleep-training method, gym membership, or potty-training regimen worked for you. "All you gotta do is *XYZ*, and you can be happy like me!" But just because you've found your wonder thing or successful solution to your problem, it doesn't mean it will work for someone else.

Eating Glass

A woman asked Chloe how her kids were sleeping. "Not great," she said. "My oldest still wakes up three times a night." The woman told her that she believed that not sleep-training babies was the equivalent of letting them swallow shards of glass. However, the woman did not know that one of Chloe's children had just undergone a sleep study that showed that he woke up twenty-four times per night from sleep apnea due to large tonsils. While sleep training was beneficial for that woman's family, it was not the answer for Chloe's. Although Chloe was upset by the comment, by the next day she had realized that the mom had not made the comment to be mean — she was just sharing her passion.

TRY THIS

If you've ever touted your cure-all to someone else, reflect on how the other person reacted.

100 Be Authentic

If we can share our story with someone who responds with empathy and understanding, shame can't survive. — BRENÉ BROWN

Share funny, proud, or beautiful yes moments with friends. Share the hard stuff, too: "I'm at my wit's end about this thing my child is doing. I don't know what to try" or "I'm feeling down about my job today." Be honest about the challenges you're encountering so you can receive the support that true friends naturally want to give. Be open with friends about your struggles and vulnerabilities.

Laundry Mountains

One playgroup made it a condition of membership for every family to have a pile of unfolded, unsorted laundry visible in their house somewhere. They could have other things going on as well — like dirty dishes in the sink, toy clutter, or dried-up toothpaste stains on their

sinks — but one visible mountain of unfolded laundry was required. This was the most active playgroup in the area, because parents knew they did not need to make their homes look pristine just to have a few people over.

TRY THIS

Name one way you feel a need to appear to have it all together around certain friends.

101 Let Friends Inspire You

One friend may be awesome in the way she lets her kids take risks, climb trees, and be independent. Another may be highly creative, always helping his kids turn their couch into a spaceship or make furry monsters out of egg cartons. Another may be amazing in the organized way she whips up Crock-Pot dinners, bakes zucchini muffins, packs day care bags, and does the dishes in twenty minutes while her children eat breakfast. Another friend may have a burgeoning vegetable garden and make spectacular soups for her kids out of exotic veggies. Another may be courageous in letting her son attend soccer camp even though he has an incurable heart condition. From friends, you may learn of great phrases, music albums, special ways to read books, herbs to put in your salad, or a new nature center. Entering friendships with the question "What can I learn from this person?" is a good place to begin.

Running Wild

Tanya, a young mom who struggled with anxiety, attended a music class with her toddler where she met a lighthearted woman with a fantastic sense of humor. The new friends let their toddlers run wild in the sprinkler and slurp dripping Popsicles while the moms talked about travel. This friend was the perfect teacher to show Tanya how to enjoy her son without having an agenda, worrying, or hovering.

TRY THIS

Think of a parent or other friend you admire. What do you learn from them?

Epilogue

The skills of parenthood are complex. They include the ability to:

- acknowledge and appreciate what you've got
- put effort into your treasured relationships
- dream about and visualize what you want
- capture magic and grace
- notice and emulate mentors
- consciously feed your own joy
- forgive yourself and others
- avoid getting too attached to things, ideas, or outcomes
- be playful and have fun
- be present and listen
- intuit knowledge, not just learn it from books
- accept and cherish what is
- notice when changes are needed and make them

- know yourself, including strengths and triggers or weak spots
- maintain priorities, even in the midst of pain or chaos

Modern parenting invites us to develop skills that are rooted in relationship, presence, and joy. Parenthood propels our growth by teaching us how to savor and stay awake to our lives, even when things are hard. It doesn't matter if you're wearing a grown-up snowsuit, donning mismatched mittens, or driving a grubby mini-van. What we're all trying to figure out is how to carve out our new identity after having kids — as parents, as people — so we can live lives we're proud of, lives of connection and joy.

Acknowledgments

I am deeply grateful to all the people who encouraged me and helped me, including my friends Andrea Berg, Beth Bodan, Erica Mayborne, and Dorothy Larsen; my sisters, Tammy Miller, Moira Staggs, and Sheilah Wasielewski; my mentors and master encouragers, America Martinez, Nancy Floy, Therese Rowley, Kay Gardner, John Douglas, Sonia Choquette, Paul Holinger, and Tabby Biddle; my honest and thorough copyeditor, Erika Büky; and my terrific writing coach, Alicia Shively. I especially thank Regina Ryan, my patient dynamo of an agent, and Jason Gardner, my supportive, wise, affable editor.

References

Action for Children Media. 2015. "Quarter of Parents Feel 'Cut Off' and Lonely." www.actionforchildren.org.uk/news-and-opinion/latest-news/2015/august /quarter-of-parents-feel-cut-off-and-lonely/.

Algoe, Sara. 2012. "Find, Remind, and Bind: The Functions of Gratitude in Everyday Relationships." *Social and Personality Psychology Compass* 6, no. 6: 455–69. Retrieved from http://cds.web.unc.edu/files/2015/03/Algoe_2012_find -remind-bind.pdf.

Algoe, Sara, Shelly Gable, and Natalya Maisel. 2010. "It's the Little Things: Everyday Gratitude as a Booster Shot for Romantic Relationships." *Personal Relationships* 17: 217–33. greatergood.berkeley.edu/images/application_uploads /Algoe-GratitudeAndRomance.pdf.

Altman, Donald. 2014. *The Mindfulness Toolbox*. Eau Claire, WI: PESI Publishing and Media.

American Psychological Association. 2007. "What Makes a Good Leader: The Assertiveness Quotient." February 4. www.apa.org/news/press/releases /2007/02/good-leaders.aspx.

Baikie, Karen, Liesbeth Geerligs, and Kay Wilhelm. 2012. "Expressive Writing and Positive Writing for Participants with Mood Disorders: An Online Randomized Control Trial." *Journal of Affective Disorders* 136, no. 3: 310–19. www.sciencedirect.com/science/article/pii/S016503271100749X.

Barnett, Lynn. 1984. "Research Note: Young Children's Resolution of Distress through Play." *Journal of Child Psychology and Psychiatry* 25, no. 3: 477–83. onlinelibrary.wiley.com/doi/10.1111/j.1469-7610.1984.tb00165.x/full.

Barton, Allen, Ted Futris, and Robert Nielsen. 2015. "Linking Financial Distress to Marital Quality: The Intermediary Roles of Demand/Withdraw and Spousal Gratitude Expressions." *Personal Relationships* 22, no. 3 (September 6): 536–49. onlinelibrary.wiley.com/doi/10.1111/pere.12094/abstract.

Barton, Jo, and Jules Pretty. 2010. "What Is the Best Dose of Nature and Green Exercise for Improving Mental Health? A Multi-study Analysis." *Environmental Science and Technology* 44, no. 10 (May 15): 3947–55. www.ncbi.nlm.nih .gov/pubmed/20337470.

Beck, Julie. 2015. "How Friendships Change in Adulthood." *The Atlantic*. October 22. www.theatlantic.com/health/archive/2015/10/how-friendships -change-over-time-in-adulthood/411466/.

Bertin, Mark. 2015. "Mindfulness Meditation: Guided Practices." *Mindful*, November 9. www.mindful.org/mindfulness-meditation-guided-practices/.

Beyer, Kristen, Andrea Kaltenbach, Aniko Szabo, Sandra Bogar, F. Javier Nieto, and Kristen Malecki. 2014. "Exposure to Neighborhood Green Space and Mental Health: Evidence from the Survey of the Health of Wisconsin." *International Journal of Environmental Research and Public Health* 11, no. 3 (March): 3453–72. www.ncbi.nlm.nih.gov/pmc/articles/PMC3987044/.

Borchard, Therese. N.d. "Words Can Change Your Brain." *Psych Central*, psych central.com/blog/archives/2013/11/30/words-can-change-your-brain/.

Borgonovi, Francesca. 2008. "Doing Well by Doing Good: The Relationship between Formal Volunteering and Self-Reported Health and Happiness." *Social Science and Medicine* 66, no. 11 (March). sciencedirect.com/science/article /pii/S0277953608000373.

Bowers, Matthew, B. Christine Green, Florian Hemme, and Laurence Chalip. 2014. "Assessing the Relationship between Youth Sport Participation Settings and Creativity in Adulthood." *Creativity Research Journal* 26, no. 3 (August 8): 314–27. www.tandfonline.com/doi/abs/10.1080/10400419.2014.929420.

Brach, Tara. 2015. "Allow Life to Be Just As It Is." *Flow Mindfulness Magazine* (English edition) July. www.tarabrach.com/wp-content/uploads/pdf/Flow _Mindfulness-Interview_Tara_Brach.pdf.

Bratman, Gregory, J. Paul Hamilton, Kevin Hahn, Gretchen Daily, and James Gross. 2015. "Nature Experience Reduces Rumination and Subgenual Prefrontal Cortex Activation." *Proceedings of the National Academy of Sciences of the United States of America* 112, no. 28 (July): 8567–72. www.pnas.org /content/112/28/8567.abstract.

Brown, Brené. 2013. "Shame v. Guilt." *Brené Brown* (blog). January 14. brenebrown .com/2013/01/14/2013114shame-v-guilt-html/.

Brown, Genevieve. 2016. "This Mom Threw Out Her Kids' Toys and Got Her Life

Back." *ABC News*. September 27. abcnews.go.com/Lifestyle/mom-threw-kids
-toys-life-back/story?id=42396129.

Bryant, Fred, and Joseph Veroff. 2007. *Savoring: A New Model of Positive Experience*. Mahwah, NJ: Lawrence Erlbaum Associates.

Burke, Moira, Cameron Marlow, and Thomas Lento. 2010. "Social Network Activity and Social Well-Being." *Proceedings of the SIGCHI Conference on Human
Factors in Computing Systems*, 1909–12. dl.acm.org/citation.cfm?doid
=1753326.1753613.

Burton, Chad, and Laura King. 2004. "The Health Benefits of Writing about
Intensely Positive Experiences." *Journal of Research in Personality* 38, no. 2
(April): 150–63. www.sciencedirect.com/science/article/pii/S0092656603
000588.

Chick, Garry, Careen Yarnal, and Andrew Purrington. 2012. "Play and Mate Preference: Testing the Signal Theory of Adult Playfulness." *American Journal of
Play* 4, no. 4 (Spring): 407–40. www.journalofplay.org/sites/www.journal
ofplay.org/files/pdf-articles/4-4-article-chick-play-and-mate-preference.pdf.

Childre, Doc, and Deborah Rozman. 2005. *Transforming Stress: The Heartmath
Solution for Relieving Worry, Fatigue, and Tension*. Oakland, CA: New Harbinger Publications.

Child Trends Databank. 2002. "Parental Warmth and Affection." www.childtrends
.org/?indicators=parental-warmth-and-affection.

Chödrön, Pema. 1994. *Start Where You Are: A Compassionate Guide to Living*. Boston: Shambhala Publications.

Cirillo, Jasmin. 2004. "Communication by Unvoiced Speech." *Annals of the Brazil-
ian Academy of Sciences* 76, no. 2: 1–11. web.fu-berlin.de/behavioral-biology
/themen/g_team/jasmin_cirillo_g003/Ref5_Communication_by_unvoiced
_speech.pdf.

Cliff, Martha. 2015. "Three-Quarters of Couples Go to Bed at Different Times due
to Heavy Workloads, Hectic Social Lives and Surfing the Web (and a Third
Admits It Causes Arguments)." *Daily Mail*. June 1. www.dailymail.co.uk
/femail/article-3105508/Three-quarters-couples-bed-different-times-heavy
-workloads-hectic-social-lives-surfing-web.html#ixzz4DHXfTMtl.

Cohen, Lawrence. 2002. *Playful Parenting*. New York: Ballantine Books.

Colino, Stacey. 2016. "Are You Catching Other People's Emotions?" *U.S. News and
World Report*. January 20. health.usnews.com/health-news/health-wellness
/articles/2016-01-20/are-you-catching-other-peoples-emotions.

Compan, E., J. Moreno, and E. Pascual. 2001. *Doing Things Together: Adolescent
Health and Family Rituals*. www.iaf-alicante.es/imgs/ckfinder/files/PUB
_Doing_things_together.pdf.

Couples Training Institute. N.d. "Gottman Couples and Marital Therapy:

Background." couplestraininginstitute.com/gottman-couples-and-marital
-therapy/. Accessed November 28, 2016.

Daily Mail Reporter. 2014. "The Secret to a Happy Marriage: Tell Your Partner
'I Love You' At Least 10 Times a Week and Go On At Least 3 Dates Every
Month." February 11. www.dailymail.co.uk/news/article-2557336/The-secret
-happy-marriage-Tell-partner-I-love-10-times-week-three-dates-month.html.

De Bloom, Jessica, Sabine Geurts, and Michiel Kompier. 2012. "Vacation (After-)
Effects on Employee Health and Well-Being, and the Role of Vacation Activ-
ities, Experiences, and Sleep." *Journal of Happiness Studies*, published online
May 12. http://link.springer.com/article/10.1007/s10902-012-9345-3.

De Jong, Peter, and Insoo Kim Berg. 2012. *Interviewing for Solutions, Fourth Edition.*
Pacific Grove, CA: Brooks/Cole.

Delamater, Ronald, and J. Regis Mcnamara. 1986. "The Social Impact of Assertiveness." *Behavior Modification* 10, no. 2: 139–58. bmo.sagepub.com/content
/10/2/139.abstract.

Denes, Amanda. 2012. "Pillow Talk: Exploring Disclosures after Sexual Activity."
Western Journal of Communication 76, no. 2 (March): 91–108. www.research
gate.net/publication/241748397_Pillow_Talk_Exploring_Disclosures_After
_Sexual_Activity.

De Vries, Dian, and Rinaldo Kuhne. 2015. "Facebook and Self-Perception: Individual Susceptibility to Negative Social Comparison on Facebook." *Personality
and Individual Differences* 86 (November): 217–21. www.sciencedirect.com
/science/article/pii/S0191886915003682.

Dishongh, Kimberly. 2015. "Study Finds Having Kids Do Chores Is a Good
Thing." *Washington Times.* July 12. www.washingtontimes.com/news/2015
/jul/12/study-finds-having-kids-do-chores-is-a-good-thing/.

Doss, Brian, Galena Rhoades, Scott Stanley, and Howard Markman. 2009. "The Effect of the Transition to Parenthood on Relationship Quality: An 8-Year Pro-
spective Study." *Journal of Personality and Social Psychology* 96, no. 3 (March):
601–19. www.ncbi.nlm.nih.gov/pubmed/19254107.

Duggan, Maeve, Amanda Lenhart, Cliff Lampe, and Nicole Ellison. 2015. *Parents
and Social Media.* Pew Research Center. July 16. www.pewinternet.org
/2015/07/16/parents-and-social-media/.

Dunifon, Rachel, and Ashish Bajracharya. 2012. "The Role of Grandparents in the
Lives of Youth." *Journal of Family Issues* 33, no. 9 (September): 1168–94.
www.ncbi.nlm.nih.gov/pmc/articles/PMC3462462/.

Emmons, Robert, and Michael McCullough. 2003. "Counting Blessings versus Bur-
dens: An Experimental Investigation of Gratitude and Subjective Well-Being
in Daily Life." *Journal of Personality and Social Psychology* 84, no. 2 (February): 377–89. dx.doi.org/10.1037/0022-3514.84.2.377.

Emmons, Robert, and Robin Stern. 2013. "Gratitude as a Psychotherapeutic

Intervention." *Journal of Clinical Psychology* 69, no. 8: 846–55. ei.yale.edu/wp-content/uploads/2013/11/jclp22020.pdf.

Entin, Esther. 2011. "All Work and No Play: Why Your Kids Are More Anxious, Depressed." *The Atlantic*. October 12. www.theatlantic.com/health/archive/2011/10/all-work-and-no-play-why-your-kids-are-more-anxious-depressed/246422/.

Erikson, Erik. 1963. *Childhood and Society*. New York: Norton.

Exline, Julie, and Roy Baumeister. 2000. "Expressing Forgiveness and Repentance: Benefits and Barriers." In *Forgiveness: Theory, Research, and Practice*, edited by Michael McCullough, Kenneth Pargament, and Carl Thoresen, 133–55. New York: Guilford.

Exline, Julie, and Peter Hill. 2012. "Humility: A Consistent and Robust Predictor of Generosity." *Journal of Positive Psychology* 7, no. 3: 208–18. www.tandfonline.com/doi/abs/10.1080/17439760.2012.671348.

Fairbrother, Nichole, Patricia Janssen, Martin Antony, Emma Tucker, and Allan Young. 2016. "Perinatal Anxiety Disorder Prevalence and Treatment." *Journal of Affective Disorders* 200: 148–55. www.jad-journal.com/article/S0165-0327(15)31132-0/abstract.

Faraut, Brice, Samir Nakib, Catherine Drogou, Maxime Elbaz, Fabien Sauvet, Jean-Pascal de Bandt, and Damien Leger. 2015. "Napping Reverses the Salivary Interleukin-6 and Urinary Norepinephrine Changes Induced by Sleep Restriction." *Journal of Clinical Endocrinology and Metabolism*, published online February 10. press.endocrine.org/doi/10.1210/jc.2014-2566.

Feeney, Brooke, and Nancy Collins. 2015. "A New Look at Social Support: A Theoretical Perspective on Thriving through Relationships." *Personality and Social Psychology Review* 19, no. 2 (May): 113–47. psr.sagepub.com/content/19/2/113.

Ferguson, Yuna. 2013. "Trying to Be Happier Really Can Work: Two Experimental Studies." *Journal of Positive Psychology* 8, no. 1: 23–33. www.tandfonline.com/doi/pdf/10.1080/17439760.2012.747000%20.

Fiese, Barbara, Kimberly Foley, and Mary Spagnola. 2006. "Routine and Ritual Elements in Family Meal Time." *New Directions in Child and Adolescent Development* 111 (Spring): 67–89. onlinelibrary.wiley.com/doi/10.1002/cd.156/abstract.

Fincham, Frank, Julie Hall, and Steven Beach. 2006. "Forgiveness in Marriage: Current Status and Future Directions." *Family Relations* 55, no. 4 (October): 415–27. onlinelibrary.wiley.com/doi/10.1111/j.1741-3729.2005.callf.x-ii/abstract.

Findley, Dane. 2014. "Joy Research Reveals What Makes People Happy." *Life Quality Examiner* (blog). February 27. lifequalityexaminer.com/joy-research-what-makes-people-happy/.

Fredrickson, Barbara. 2004. "The Broaden-and-Build Theory of Positive Emo-
    tions." *Philosophical Transactions of the Royal Society B 359* (September):
    1367–77. doi: 10.1098/rstb.2004.1512.

Froh, Jeffrey, Christopher Fives, Ryan Fuller, Matthew Jacofsky, Mark Terjesen,
    and Charles Yurkewicz. 2007. "Interpersonal Relationships and Irrationality as
    Predictors of Life Satisfaction." *Journal of Positive Psychology* 2, no. 1: 29–39.
    www.tandfonline.com/doi/abs/10.1080/17439760601069051.

Gabb, Jacqui, Martina Klett-Davies, Janet Fink, and Manuela Thomae. 2013. "En-
    during Love? Couple Relationships in the 21st Century: Survey Findings Re-
    port." Open University. November. www.open.ac.uk/researchprojects
    /enduringlove/sites/www.open.ac.uk.researchprojects.enduringlove/files
    /files/ecms/web-content/Final-Enduring-Love-Survey-Report.pdf.

Giallo, Rebecca, Natalie Rose, Amanda Cooklin, and Derek McCormack. 2012. "In
    Survival Mode: Mothers' and Fathers' Experiences of Fatigue in the Early Par-
    enting Period." *Journal of Reproductive and Infant Psychology* 31, no. 1: 31–45.
    www.tandfonline.com/doi/abs/10.1080/02646838.2012.751584.

Gillespie, Brian, David Frederick, Lexi Harari, and Christian Grov. 2015. "Ho-
    mophily, Close Friendship, and Life Satisfaction among Gay, Lesbian, Hetero-
    sexual, and Bisexual Men and Women." *PLOS ONE* 10, no. 6 (June): 601–19.
    journals.plos.org/plosone/article?id=10.1371/journal.pone.0128900.

Girme, Yuthika, Nickola Overall, and Sivailele Faingataa. 2014. "'Date Nights,'
    Take Two: The Maintenance Function of Shared Relationship Activities."
    Personal Relationships (March): 125–49. onlinelibrary.wiley.com/doi/10.1111
    /pere.12020/abstract.

Goldstein, Andrea, and Matthew Walker. 2014. "The Role of Sleep in Emotional
    Brain Function." *Annual Review of Clinical Psychology.* Published online Janu-
    ary 31. www.ncbi.nlm.nih.gov/pmc/articles/PMC4286245/.

Goleman, Daniel. 1991. "Happy or Sad, a Mood Can Prove Contagious." *New York
    Times.* October 15. www.nytimes.com/1991/10/15/science/happy-or-sad-a
    -mood-can-prove-contagious.html.

———. 1992. "Family Rituals May Promote Better Emotional Adjustment." *New
    York Times.* March 11. www.nytimes.com/1992/03/11/news/family-rituals
    -may-promote-better-emotional-adjustment.html.

Gollwitzer, Peter. 1999. "Implementation Intentions: Strong Effects of Simple
    Plans." *American Psychologist* 54, no. 7 (July): 493–503. www.psych.nyu.edu
    /gollwitzer/99Goll_ImpInt.pdf.

Gordon, Amie. 2010. "When You Accept Me for Me: The Relational Benefits of
    Intrinsic Affirmations from One's Relationship Partner." *Personality and Social
    Psychology Bulletin* 36, no. 11: 1439–53, psp.sagepub.com/content/36
    /11/1439.

———. 2016. "How to Save Your Marriage from Parenthood." Greater Good

Science Center. July 20. greatergood.berkeley.edu/article/item/how_to
_save_your_marriage_from_parenthood.

Gordon, Amie, Emily Impett, Aleksandr Kogan, Christopher Oveis, and Dacher
Keltner. 2012. "To Have and to Hold: Gratitude Promotes Relationship Main-
tenance in Intimate Bonds." *Journal of Personality and Social Psychology* 103,
no. 2 (May): 257–74.

Gore, Julie, and Eugene Sadler-Smith. 2011. "Unpacking Intuition." *General Psychology* 15, no. 4 (December): 304–16. www.epubs.surrey.ac.uk/791731/2
/GoreSadlerSmith2011RGP.pdf.

Gottman, John. 2015. "The Empirical Basis for Gottman Method Couples Therapy." Blog post. Gottman Institute. June 24. www.gottman.com/blog/the
-empirical-basis-for-gottman-method-couples-therapy/.

Gottman Institute. 2013. "The Empirical Basis for Gottman Couples Therapy."
www.gottman.com/wp-content/uploads/EmpiricalBasis-Update3.pdf.

Goudreau, Jenna. 2015. "A Mathematical Formula Reveals the Secret to Lasting
Relationships." *Business Insider*. June 29. www.businessinsider.com
/mathematical-secret-to-lasting-relationships-2015-6.

Goyal, Madhav, Sonal Singh, Erica Sibinga, Neda Gould, Anastasia Rowland-
Seymour, Ritu Sharma, Zackary Berger, et al. 2014. "Meditation Programs
for Psychological Stress and Well-Being: A Systematic Review and Meta-
analysis." *JAMA Internal Medicine* 174, no. 3: 357–68. archinte.jamanetwork
.com/article.aspx?articleid=1809754.

Gray, Peter. 2011. "The Decline of Play and the Rise of Psychopathology in Children and Adolescents." *American Journal of Play* 3, no. 4. www.journalofplay
.org/sites/www.journalofplay.org/files/pdf-articles/3-4-article-gray-decline
-of-play.pdf.

Greenspan Floortime Approach. 2015. "About Floortime." www.stanleygreenspan
.com/about-floortime.

Gueguen, Nicolas, and Jordy Stefan. 2016. "'Green Altruism': Short Immersion in
Natural Green Environments and Helping Behavior." *Environment and Behavior* 48, no. 2 (February): 324–42. eab.sagepub.com/content/48/2/324.abstract.

Gupta, Uma, and B. S. Gupta. 2016. "Gender Differences in Psychophysiological
Responses to Music Listening." *Music and Medicine* 8, no. 1: 53–64. mmd
.iammonline.com/index.php/musmed/article/viewFile/471/308.

Hall, James. 2012. "Children Prefer Simple Pleasures to Organized Trips, Research
Finds." *Telegraph*. August 17. www.telegraph.co.uk/finance/newsbysector
/retailandconsumer/9480785/Children-prefer-simple-pleasures-to-organised
-trips-research-finds.html.

Hancock, Kirsten, Nadia Cunningham, David Lawrence, David Zarb, and Stephen
Zubrick. 2015. "Playgroup Participation and Social Support Outcomes for

Mothers of Young Children: A Longitudinal Cohort Study." *PLOS ONE* 10, no. 7. journals.plos.org/plosone/article?id=10.1371/journal.pone.0133007.

Harmon, Katherine. 2010. "How Important Is Physical Contact with Your Infant?" *Scientific American*. May. www.scientificamerican.com/article/infant-touch/.

Harris, Malcolm. 2016. "The Privatization of Childhood Play." *Pacific Standard*. May 12. psmag.com/the-privatization-of-childhood-play-956b02c154d3# .0w63ey6b1.

Hart, Betty, and Todd Risley. 2003. "The Early Catastrophe: The 30 Million Word Gap by Age 3." *American Educator* (Spring): 4–9. www.aft.org//sites/default /files/periodicals/TheEarlyCatastrophe.pdf.

Harvard Mental Health Letter. 2011. "In Praise of Gratitude." November. www .health.harvard.edu/newsletter_article/in-praise-of-gratitude.

Hasler, Brant, and Wendy Troxel. 2010. "Couples' Nighttime Sleep Efficiency and Concordance: Evidence for Bidirectional Associations with Daytime Relationship Functioning." *Psychosomatic Medicine* 72, no. 8 (October): 794–801. www.ncbi.nlm.nih.gov/pmc/articles/PMC2950886/.

Hatfield, Elaine, Lisamarie Bensman, Paul Thornton, and Richard Rapson. 2014. "New Perspectives on Emotional Contagion: A Review of Classic and Recent Research on Facial Mimicry and Contagion." *Interpersona* 8, no. 2: 159–79. interpersona.psychopen.eu/article/view/162/html.

Hobson, Tom. 2015. "Stupid Questions." *Teacher Tom* (blog). July 28. teachertoms blog.blogspot.com/2015/07/stupid-questions.html.

Hodges, Timothy, and Donald Clifton. 2004. "Strengths-Based Development in Practice." In *Positive Psychology in Practice*, edited by Alex Linley and Shane Joseph. Hoboken, NJ: John Wiley and Sons.

Hoffman, Adam. 2015. "What Does a Grateful Brain Look Like?" Greater Good Science Center. November 16. greatergood.berkeley.edu/article/item/what _does_a_grateful_brain_look_like.

Holt-Lunstad, Julianne, Timothy Smith, and J. Bradley Layton. 2010. "Social Relationships and Mortality Risk: A Meta-analytic Review." *PLOS Med* 7, no. 7 (July). journals.plos.org/plosmedicine/article?id=10.1371/journal .pmed.1000316.

Holzel, Britta, James Carmody, Mark Vangel, Christina Congleton, Sita Yerramsetti, Tim Gard, and Sara Lazar. 2011. "Mindfulness Practice Leads to Increases in Regional Brain Gray Matter Density." *Psychiatry* 19, no. 1: 36–43. www.ncbi.nlm.nih.gov/pubmed/21071182.

Immordino-Yang, Mary Helen, Joanna Christodoulou, and Vanessa Singh. 2012. "Rest Is Not Idleness." *Perspectives on Psychological Science* 7, no. 4 (July): 352–64. pps.sagepub.com/content/7/4/352.

Johnston, Wendy, and Graham Davey. 1997. "The Psychological Impact of Negative TV News Bulletins." *British Journal of Psychology* 88, no. 1 (February):

85–91. onlinelibrary.wiley.com/doi/10.1111/j.2044-8295.1997.tb02622.x
/abstract.

Jordan, Alexander, Benoit Monin, Carol Dweck, Benjamin Lovett, Oliver John, and
James Gross. 2011. "Misery Has More Company than People Think: Underes-
timating the Prevalence of Others' Negative Emotions." *Personality and Social
Psychology Bulletin* 37, no. 1: 120–35. http://psp.sagepub.com/content/37
/1/120.abstract.

Karr-Morse, Robin, and Meredith Wiley. 2012. *Scared Sick: The Role of Childhood
Trauma in Adult Disease*. New York: Basic Books.

Kelley, Barbara, and Shannon Kelley. 2012. "A Fine Mess: Why We Need to Ditch
the Clutter." *Huffington Post*. July 9. www.huffingtonpost.com/shannon-kelley
/clutter_b_1656670.html.

Keltner, Dacher. 2010a. *Dacher Keltner on Touch*. Video. www.youtube.com/watch
?v=GW5p8xOVwRo.

———. 2010b. *Hands-On Research: The Science of Touch*. Greater Good Science
Center. September 29. greatergood.berkeley.edu/article/item/hands_on
_research.

Keng, Shian-Ling, Moria Smoski, and Clive Robins. 2011. "Effects of Mindfulness
on Psychological Health: A Review of Empirical Studies." *Clinical Psychology
Review* 31, no. 6 (August): 1041–56. www.ncbi.nlm.nih.gov/pmc/articles
/PMC3679190/.

Killingsworth, Matthew, and Daniel Gilbert. 2010. "A Wandering Mind is an Unhappy Mind." *Science* 330, no. 6006 (November 12). science.sciencemag.org
/content/330/6006/932.

Knapton, Sarah. 2015. "Boredom Makes People More Creative, Claim Psychologists."
Telegraph. March 25. www.telegraph.co.uk/news/science/science-news
/11492867/Boredom-makes-people-more-creative-claim-psychologists.html.

Kochanska, Grazyna, and Sanghag Kim. 2013. "Early Attachment Organization
with Both Parents and Future Behavior Problems: From Infancy to Middle
Childhood." *Child Development* 84, no. 1 (January–February): 283–96.
www.ncbi.nlm.nih.gov/pubmed/23005703.

Krejtz, Izabela, John Nezlek, Anna Michnicka, Pawel Holas, and Marzena Rusa-
nowska. 2016. "Counting One's Blessings Can Reduce the Impact of Daily
Stress." *Journal of Happiness Studies* 17, no. 1 (February): 25–39. link.springer
.com/article/10.1007/s10902-014-9578-4.

Kross, Ethan, Jiyoung Park, Adrienne Dougherty, Holly Shablack, Ryan Bremner,
Emma Bruehlman-Senecal, Jason Moser, and Ozlem Ayduk. 2014. "Self-Talk
as a Regulatory Mechanism: How You Do It Matters." *Journal of Personality
and Social Psychology* 106, no. 2: 304–24. selfcontrol.psych.lsa.umich.edu
/wp-content/uploads/2014/01/KrossJ_Pers_Soc_Psychol2014Self-talk
_as_a_regulatory_mechanism_How_you_do_it_matters.pdf.

Kross, Ethan, Philippe Verduyn, Emre Demiralp, Jiyoung Park, David Seungiae Lee, Natalie Lin, Holly Shablack, John Jonides, and Oscar Ybarra. 2013. "Facebook Use Predicts Declines in Subjective Well-Being in Young Adults." *PLOS ONE* 8, no. 8. journals.plos.org/plosone/article?id=10.1371/journal .pone.0069841.

Kulur, Anupama, Nagaraja Haleagrahara, Prabha Adhikary, and P. S. Jeganathan. 2009. "Effect of Diaphragmatic Breathing on Heart Rate Variability in Ischemic Heart Disease with Diabetes." *Arquivos Brasileiros de Cardiologia* 92, no. 6 (June): 423–29. www.scielo.br/scielo.php?script=sci_arttext&pid =S0066-782X2009000600008&lng=pt&nrm=iso&tlng=pt.

Kuo, Frances, and Andrea Taylor. 2004. "A Potential Natural Treatment for Attention-Deficit/Hyperactivity Disorder: Evidence from a National Study." *American Journal of Public Health* 94, no. 9 (September): 1580–86. www.ncbi .nlm.nih.gov/pmc/articles/PMC1448497/.

Lai, Siew. 2014. "The Efficacy of Gratitude Practice on Well-Being: A Randomized Controlled Trial." MSc Thesis, University of Stirling. www.stir.ac.uk/media /schools/is/files/LaiMSc2014.pdf.

Lally, Maria. 2016. "Say Hello to Hygge: The Danish Secret to Happiness." *Telegraph*. August 27. www.telegraph.co.uk/women/life/say-hello-to-hygge -the-danish-secret-to-happiness/.

Lamott, Anne. 2015. "I Am Going to Be 61 Years Old in 48 Hours." Facebook post. @AnneLamott. April 8. www.facebook.com/AnneLamott/posts /662177577245222.

Lansbury, Janet. 2014a. "Play Space Inspiration." *Janet Lansbury* (blog). August 14. www.janetlansbury.com/2014/08/play-space-inspiration/.

———. 2014b. "4 Toddler Testing Behaviors (and How to Cope)." *Janet Lansbury* (blog). July 31. www.janetlansbury.com/2014/07/4-toddler-testing-behaviors -and-how-to-cope/.

Larson, Jeffry D., Russell Crane, and Craig Smith. 1991. "Morning and Night Couples: The Effect of Wake and Sleep Patterns on Marital Adjustment." *Journal of Marital and Family Therapy* 17, no. 1 (January): 53–65. onlinelibrary.wiley .com/doi/10.1111/j.1752-0606.1991.tb00864.x/abstract.

Ledbetter, Andrew M., Em Griffin, and Glenn G. Sparks. 2007. "Forecasting 'Friends Forever': A Longitudinal Investigation of Sustained Closeness between Best Friends." *Personal Relationships* 14, no. 2 (June): 343–50. online library.wiley.com/doi/10.1111/j.1475–6811.2007.00158.x/full.

Lisitsa, Ellie. 2012. "The Positive Perspective: Dr. Gottman's Magic Ratio!" *Gottman Relationship Blog*. December 5. www.gottman.com/blog/the-positive -perspective-dr-gottmans-magic-ratio/.

Longhi, Elena. 2013. "Wellbeing and Hospitalized Children: Can Music Help?" *Psychology of Music* (August). pom.sagepub.com/content/early/2013/08/22 /0305735613499781.abstract.

Luby, Joan, Andy Belden, Kelly Botteron, Natasha Marrus, Michael Harms, Casey Babb, Tomoyuki Nishino, and Deanna Barch. 2013. "The Effects of Poverty on Childhood Brain Development: The Mediating Effect of Caregiving and Stressful Life Events." *JAMA Pediatrics* 167, no. 12: 1135–42. archpedi.jama network.com/article.aspx?articleid=1761544.

Manczak, Erika, Anita DeLongis, and Edith Chen. 2016. "Does Empathy Have a Cost? Diverging Psychological and Physiological Effects within Families." *Health Psychology* 35, no. 3 (March): 211–18. psycnet.apa.org/journals/hea /35/3/211/.

Margolis, Rachel, and Mikko Myrskyla. 2015. "Parental Well-Being Surrounding First Birth as a Determinant of Further Parity Progression." *Demography* 52, no. 4: 1147–66.

McGlinchey, Eleanor, Lisa Talbot, Keng-hao Chang, Katherine Kaplan, Ronald Dahl, and Allison Harvey. 2011. "The Effect of Sleep Deprivation on Vocal Expression of Emotion in Adolescents and Adults." *Sleep* 34, no. 9: 1233–41. www.ncbi.nlm.nih.gov/pmc/articles/PMC3157665/.

McKay, James. 2012. "The Effects of Diaphragmatic Breathing on College Student Stress." Thesis, Carroll College.

Mead, M. Nathaniel. 2008. "Benefits of Sunlight: A Bright Spot for Human Health." *Environmental Health Perspectives* 116, no. 4 (April): A160–70. www.ncbi .nlm.nih.gov/pmc/articles/PMC2290997/.

Minkel, Jared, Siobhan Banks, Oo Htaik, Marisa Moreta, Christopher Jones, Eleanor McGlinchey, Norah Simpson, and David Dinges. 2012. "Sleep Deprivation and Stressors: Evidence for Elevated Negative Affect in Response to Mild Stressors When Sleep Deprived." *Emotion* 12, no. 5: 1015–20. www.ncbi .nlm.nih.gov/pmc/articles/PMC3964364/.

Montero-Marin, Jesus, Petros Skapinakis, Ricardo Araya, Margarita Gili, and Javier Garcia-Campayo. 2011. "Towards a Brief Definition of Burnout Syndrome by Subtypes: Development of the 'Burnout Clinical Subtypes Questionnaire' (BCSQ-12)," *Health and Quality of Life Outcomes* 9, no. 74. www.medscape .com/viewarticle/752519_2.

Moore, Elizabeth Armstrong. 2014. "What Is the Blue Light from Our Screens Really Doing to Our Eyes?" *Gigaom*. September 1. gigaom.com/2014/09/01 /what-is-the-blue-light-from-our-screens-really-doing-to-our-eyes/?utm _source=digg&utm_medium=email.

National Institute for Play. N.d. "The Opportunities: Relationships." www.nifplay .org/opportunities/relationships/. Accessed November 24, 2016.

Newberg, Andrew, and Mark Robert Waldman. 2013. *Words Can Change Your Brain: 12 Conversation Strategies to Build Trust, Resolve Conflict, and Increase Intimacy.* New York: Penguin.

Newman, Lareen. 2008. "How Parenthood Experiences Influence Desire for More

Children in Australia: A Qualitative Study." *Journal of Population Research* 25, no. 1 (March): 1–27. link.springer.com/article/10.1007/BF03031938.

Parnell, Kenneth. 2015. "The Influence of a Couple Gratitude Intervention on Emotions, Intimacy, and Satisfaction in the Relationship." PhD diss., University of Nebraska, Lincoln.

Patterson, Charlotte, Deborah Cohn, and Barbara Kao. 1989. "Maternal Warmth as a Protective Factor against Risk Associated with Peer Rejection among Children." *Development and Psychopathology* 1, no. 1: 21–38. www.researchgate .net/publication/231929242_Maternal_warmth_as_a_protective_factor _against_risk_associated_with_peer_rejection_among_children.

Paul, Ian, Danielle Downs, Eric Schaefer, Jessica Beiler, and Carol Weisman. 2013. "Postpartum Anxiety and Maternal-Infant Health Outcomes." *Pediatrics* 131, no. 4 (April). www.ncbi.nlm.nih.gov/pubmed/23460682.

Payne, Kim John. 2010. *Simplicity Parenting.* New York: Ballantine Books.

Perry, Keith. 2014. "Happiest Couples Sleep an Inch Apart." *Telegraph.* April 16. www.telegraph.co.uk/women/sex/10768902/Happiest-couples-sleep-an -inch-apart.html.

Poulsen, Shruti. 2008. *A Fine Balance: The Magic Ratio to a Healthy Relationship.* Purdue Extension, Consumer and Family Sciences. March. www.extension .purdue.edu/extmedia/cfs/cfs-744-w.pdf.

Rausch, Sarah, Sandra Gramling, and Stephen Auerbach. 2006. "Effects of a Single Session of Large-Group Meditation and Progressive Muscle Relaxation Training on Stress Reduction, Reactivity, and Recovery." *International Journal of Stress Management* 13, no. 3: 273–90. psycnet.apa.org/psycinfo/2006 -10511-002.

Rees, C. A. 2005. "Thinking about Children's Attachments: A Review." *Archives of Diseases in Childhood* 90: 1058–65. www.ncbi.nlm.nih.gov/pmc/articles /PMC1720124/pdf/v090p01058.pdf.

Roberts, James, and Meredith David. 2016. "My Life Has Become a Major Distraction from My Cell Phone: Partner Phubbing and Relationship Satisfaction among Romantic Partners." *Computers in Human Behavior* 54 (January): 134–41. www.sciencedirect.com/science/article/pii/S0747563215300704.

Robinson, John. 2013. "Happiness Means Being Just Rushed Enough." *Scientific American.* February. www.scientificamerican.com/article/happiness-means -being-just-rushed-enough/.

Rotkirch, Anna. 2009. "Maternal Guilt." *Evolutionary Psychology* 8, no. 1: 90–106. evp.sagepub.com/content/8/1/147470491000800108.full.pdf.

Saleebey, Dennis. 2006. "Introduction: Power in the People." In *The Strengths Perspective in Social Work Practice*, edited by Dennis Saleebey. Boston: Allyn & Bacon.

Salzberg, Sharon. 2002. *Loving-Kindness: The Revolutionary Art of Happiness.* Boston: Shambhala Classics.

Sarkova, Maria, Maria Bacikova-Sleskova, Olga Orosova, Andrea Madarasova Geckova, Zuzana Katreniakova, Daniel Klein, Wim van den Huevel, and Jitse P. van Dilk. 2013. "Associations between Assertiveness, Psychological Well-Being, and Self-Esteem in Adolescents." *Journal of Applied Social Psychology* 43, no. 1 (January): 147–54, onlinelibrary.wiley.com/doi/10.1111 /j.1559-1816.2012.00988.x/abstract.

Saxbe, D. E., and R. Repetti. 2010. "No Place Like Home: Home Tours Correlate with Daily Patterns of Mood and Cortisol." *Personal and Social Psychology Bulletin* 36, no. 1 (January): 71–81. www.ncbi.nlm.nih.gov/pubmed/19934011.

Schade, Lori, Jonathan Sandberg, Roy Bean, Dean Busby, and Sarah Coyne. 2013. "Using Technology to Connect in Romantic Relationships: Effects on Attachment, Relationship Satisfaction, and Stability in Emerging Adults." *Journal of Couple and Relationship Therapy* 12, no. 4. www.tandfonline.com/doi/abs /10.1080/15332691.2013.836051.

Schwartz, Richard. 1995. *Internal Family Systems Therapy*. New York: Guilford Press.

Science Daily. 2014. "Early Caregiving Experiences Have Long-Term Effects on Social Relationships, Achievement." December 18. www.sciencedaily.com /releases/2014/12/141218081330.htm.

Search Institute. 2005. "40 Developmental Assets for Early Childhood." www .search-institute.org/system/files/a/40AssetsList_3-5_Eng.pdf.

Seligman, Martin, Tracy Steen, Nansook Park, and Christopher Peterson. 2005. "Positive Psychology Progress: Empirical Validation of Interventions." *American Psychology* 60, no. 5 (July–August): 410–21. www.ncbi.nlm.nih.gov /pubmed/16045394.

Senior, Jennifer. 2010. "All Joy and No Fun: Why Parents Hate Parenting." *New York Magazine*. July 4. nymag.com/news/features/67024/.

Seppälä, Emma. 2014. "18 Science-Based Reasons to Try Loving Kindness Meditation." *Mindful*. October 1. www.mindful.org/18-science-based-reasons-to -try-loving kindness-meditation/.

Singer, Dorothy, Jerome Singer, Heidi D'Agostino, and Raeka DeLong. 2009. "Children's Pastimes and Play in Sixteen Nations: Is Free-Play Declining?" *American Journal of Play* (Winter). www.journalofplay.org/sites/www.journal ofplay.org/files/pdf-articles/1-3-article-childrens-pastimes-play-in-sixteen -nations.pdf.

Sirota, Karen. 2006. "Habits of the Hearth: Children's Bedtime Routines as Relational Work." *Text and Talk* 26, no. 4–5 (September): 493–514. www.research gate.net/publication/250975815_Habits_of_the_Hearth_Children%27s _Bedtime_Routines_as_Relational_Work.

Smith, Emily Esfahani. 2014. "Masters of Love." *The Atlantic*. June 12. www.the atlantic.com/health/archive/2014/06/happily-ever-after/372573/.

Smith, Jeremy Adam. 2014. "Scientific Insights from the Greater Good Gratitude

Summit." Greater Good Science Center. June 17. greatergood.berkeley.edu /article/item/new_insights_from_the_gratitude_summit.

Social Issues Research Centre. 2004. *The Flirting Report*. www.sirc.org/publik /Flirt2.pdf.

Staples, Angela, John Bates, and Isaac Petersen. 2015. "Bedtime Routines in Early Childhood: Prevalence, Consistency, and Associations with Nighttime Sleep." *Monographs of the Society for Research in Child Development* 80, no. 1: 141–59. www.ncbi.nlm.nih.gov/pubmed/25704740.

Steers, Mai-Ly, Robert Wickham, and Linda Acitelli. 2014. "Seeing Everyone Else's Highlight Reels: How Facebook Usage Is Linked to Depressive Symptoms." *Journal of Social and Clinical Psychology* 33, no. 8 (October): 701–31. guilford journals.com/doi/abs/10.1521/jscp.2014.33.8.701.

Stiffelman, Susan. 2015. "Being the Calm, Confident Captain of the Ship in Your Child's Life." *Susan Stiffelman* (blog). November 20. susanstiffelman.com /being-the-calm-confident-captain-of-the-ship-in-your-childs-life/.

———. 2012. *Parenting without Power Struggles: Raising Joyful, Resilient Kids While Staying Cool, Calm, and Connected*. New York: Simon & Schuster.

Sullivan, Bob, and Hugh Thompson. 2013. "Brain, Interrupted." *New York Times.* May 3. www.nytimes.com/2013/05/05/opinion/sunday/a-focus-on -distraction.html?_r=4.

Sullivan, Meg. 2012. "Trouble in Paradise: UCLA Book Enumerates Challenges Faced by Middle-Class L.A. Families." *UCLA Newsroom*. June 19. newsroom .ucla.edu/releases/trouble-in-paradise-new-ucla-book.

Tartakovsky, Margarita. N.d. "The Importance of Play for Adults." *Psych Central*. psychcentral.com/blog/archives/2012/11/15/the-importance-of-play-for -adults/.

Tarullo, Amanda, Jelena Obradovic, and Megan Gunnar. 2009. "Self-Control and the Developing Brain." Zero to Three (January): 31–37. web.stanford.edu /group/sparklab/pdf/Tarullo,%20Obradovic,%20Gunnar%20(2009,%20 0-3)%20Self-Control%20and%20the%20Developing%20Brain.pdf.

Tatkin, Stan. 2011. *Wired for Love*. Oakland, CA: New Harbinger Publications.

Thøgersen-Ntoumani, C., E. Loughren, F. Kinnafick, I. Taylor, J. Duda, and K. Fox. 2015. "Changes in Work Affect in Response to Lunchtime Walking in Previously Inactive Employees: A Randomized Trial." *Scandinavian Journal of Medicine and Science in Sports* 25, no. 6: 778–87. www.ncbi.nlm.nih.gov /pubmed/25559067.

Thrash, Todd M., and Andrew J. Elliot. 2004. "Inspiration: Core Characteristics, Component Processes, Antecedents, and Function." *Journal of Personality and Social Psychology* 87, no. 6: 957–973. www.ncbi.nlm.nih.gov/pubmed/15598117.

Tice, Sheerah. 2007. "The Effects of Deep Breathing and Positive Imagery on Stress and Coherence Levels among College-Age Women." Senior honors

thesis, Liberty University. http://digitalcommons.liberty.edu/cgi/view
content.cgi?article=1016&context=honors.

Tippett, Krista. 2015. "Transcript for Brené Brown: The Courage to Be Vulnerable." *On Being, with Krista Tippett.* January 29. Interview transcript. www
.onbeing.org/program/brené-brown-on-deep-shame-and-the-courage-to
-be-vulnerable/transcript/6065.

United Health Group. 2013. "Study Reveals Volunteering Makes Positive Impact on
People's Health." *News Medical.* June 19. news-medical.net/news/20130619
/Study-reveals-volunteering-makes-positive-impact-on-peoples-health.aspx.

Van Anders, Sari, Robin Edelstein, Ryan Wade, and Chelsea Samples-Steele. 2013.
"Descriptive Experiences and Sexual vs. Nurturant Aspects of Cuddling between Adult Romantic Partners." *Archives of Sexual Behavior* 42, no. 4: 553–60.
www.ncbi.nlm.nih.gov/pubmed/23070529.

Venkatraman, Rohini, and Kristen Berman. 2015. "How Can You Use Gifts to Improve Your Relationships?" *Irrational Labs* (blog). December 22. irrational
labs.org/2015/12/how-to-to-use-gifts-to-improve-your-relationships/.

Verduyn, Philippe, David Seungiae Lee, Jiyoung Park, Holly Shablack, Ariana Orvell, Joseph Bayer, Oscar Ybarra, John Jonides, and Ethan Kross. 2015. "Passive Facebook Usage Undermines Affective Well-Being: Experimental and
Longitudinal Evidence." *Journal of Experiential Psychology* 144, no. 2: 480–88.
psycnet.apa.org/index.cfm?fa=buy.optionToBuy&uid=2015-08049-001.

Waters, Sara, Tessa West, and Wendy Mendes. 2014. "Stress Contagion: Physiological Covariation between Mothers and Infants." *Psychological Science* 24, no. 4:
934–42. http://pss.sagepub.com/content/25/4/934.

Weinstein, Netta. 2009. "Can Nature Make Us More Caring? Effects of Immersion
in Nature on Intrinsic Aspirations and Generosity." *Personality and Social Psychology Bulletin* 35, no. 10 (October): 1315–29, psp.sagepub.com/content
/35/10/1315.abstract.

Wilcox, W. Bradford, and Jeffrey Dew. 2012. "The Date Night Opportunity: What
Does Couple Time Tell Us about the Potential Value of Date Nights?" National Marriage Project. nationalmarriageproject.org/wp-content/uploads
/2012/05/NMP-DateNight.pdf.

Williams, Kate, Margaret Barrett, Graham Welch, Vicky Abad, and Mary Broughton. 2015. "Associations between Early Shared Music Activities in the Home
and Later Child Outcomes: Findings from the Longitudinal Study of Australian Children." *Early Childhood Research Quarterly* 31: 113–24. www.science
direct.com/science/article/pii/S0885200615000058.

Wisner, Katherine, Dorothy Sit, Mary McShea, David Rizzo, Rebecca Zoretich,
Carolyn Hughes, Heather Eng, et al. 2013. "Onset Timing, Thoughts of Self-Harm, and Diagnoses in Postpartum Women with Screen-Positive Depression

Findings." *JAMA Psychiatry* 70, no. 5 (May): 490–98, archpsyc.jamanetwork
.com/article.aspx?articleid=1666651.

Witvliet, Charlotte, Thomas Ludwig, and Kelly Van der Laan. 2001. "Granting Forgiveness or Harboring Grudges: Implications for Emotion, Physiology, and
Health." *Psychological Science* 12, no. 2: 117–23. pss.sagepub.com/content
/12/2/117.short.

Wolpert, Stuart. 2012. "Here Is What Real Commitment to Your Marriage Means."
UCLA Newsroom. February 1. newsroom.ucla.edu/releases/here-is-what-real
-commitment-to-228064.

Worthington, Everett. 2004. "The New Science of Forgiveness." Greater Good
Science Center. September 1. greatergood.berkeley.edu/article/item/the
_new_science_of_forgiveness.

Zajicek-Farber, Michaela, Lynn Mayer, Laura Daughtery, and Erika Rodkey. 2014.
"The Buffering Effect of Childhood Routines: Longitudinal Connections between Early Parenting and Prekindergarten Learning Readiness of Children in
Low-Income Families." *Journal of Social Service Research* 40, no. 5: 699–720.
www.tandfonline.com/doi/abs/10.1080/01488376.2014.930946?journalCode
=wssr20&.

Zawadzki, Matthew, Joshua Smyth, and Heather Costigan. 2015. "Real-Time Associations between Engaging in Leisure and Daily Health and Well-Being."
Annals of Behavioral Medicine 49, no. 4 (August): 605–15.

Zero to Three. 2016. *Tuning In: National Parent Survey Overview.* Report. 1–6.
www.zerotothree.org/resources/1424-national-parent-survey-overview
-and-key-insights#downloads.

Zimmerman, Eilene. 2007. "Hobbies Are Rich in Psychic Rewards." *New York
Times.* December 2. www.nytimes.com/2007/12/02/jobs/02career
.html?_r=0.

Zyga, Lisa. 2008. "Physicists Investigate 'Best Friends Forever.'" Phys.org,
April 22. phys.org/news/2008-04-physicists-friends.html#jCp.

Index

About the Author

Erin Leyba, LCSW, PhD, is an individual and marriage counselor in private practice in Chicago's western suburbs. Dr. Leyba specializes in helping parents overcome challenges and enjoy the magical times when their children are young. She offers mini retreats to help couples reconnect after having children and workshops to help individuals to process the immense changes brought on by parenthood. She also speaks to parent groups, childcare facilities, and businesses on self-care, joy, humor, mindfulness, relationships, and compassion. Dr. Leyba has taught master's- and doctoral-level social-work courses, including child development and school social work, at the University of Chicago, Loyola University, the University of Illinois at Chicago, and the Institute for Clinical Social Work. She earned the Provost Award for her research on applications of strengths-based social work to youth development.

Dr. Leyba blogs at www.erinleyba.com, and her posts have been featured on *Psychology Today, Elephant Journal, Hello Dearest, Moms Magazine, BlogHer, Positive Parents* (Positive-parents.org), and other sites. She is available for speaking engagements and can be contacted at erinleyba@gmail.com.

NEW WORLD LIBRARY is dedicated to publishing books and other media that inspire and challenge us to improve the quality of our lives and the world.

We are a socially and environmentally aware company. We recognize that we have an ethical responsibility to our customers, our staff members, and our planet.

We serve our customers by creating the finest publications possible on personal growth, creativity, spirituality, wellness, and other areas of emerging importance. We serve New World Library employees with generous benefits, significant profit sharing, and constant encouragement to pursue their most expansive dreams.

As a member of the Green Press Initiative, we print an increasing number of books with soy-based ink on 100 percent postconsumer-waste recycled paper. Also, we power our offices with solar energy and contribute to non-profit organizations working to make the world a better place for us all.

Our products are available in bookstores everywhere.

www.newworldlibrary.com

At NewWorldLibrary.com you can download our catalog,
subscribe to our e-newsletter, read our blog,
and link to authors' websites, videos, and podcasts.

Find us on Facebook, follow us on Twitter, and watch us on YouTube.

Send your questions and comments our way!
You make it possible for us to do what we love to do.

Phone: 415-884-2100 or 800-972-6657
Catalog requests: Ext. 10 | Orders: Ext. 10 | Fax: 415-884-2199
escort@newworldlibrary.com

NEW WORLD LIBRARY
publishing books that change lives   14 Pamaron Way, Novato, CA 94949